Henry Bedford

The Life of St. Vincent de Paul

Henry Bedford

The Life of St. Vincent de Paul

THE LIFE

OF

ST. VINCENT DE PAUL.

BY

HENRY BEDFORD, M.A.

LONDON:
BURNS AND OATES.
1883.

TO

THE VERY REVEREND THE PRESIDENT,

THE REVEREND THE DIRECTORS,

AND

THE STUDENTS

OF THE

FOREIGN MISSIONARY COLLEGE OF ALLHALLOWS,

DUBLIN,

This Biography

OF THE FOUNDER OF THE CONGREGATION OF THE FATHERS OF THE MISSION

IS MOST AFFECTIONATELY INSCRIBED

BY THE AUTHOR.

PREFACE.

They who know any thing of the saintly character and heroic deeds of Vincent de Paul regard him, and with truth, as the father of the orphan, the friend of the poor man, and the tender nurse of the sick; but only they who have studied his career by the light of the times in which he lived are aware how eminently he was distinguished as a zealous and successful reformer. To him belongs the glory of raising the Church of France from the deep degradation into which it had been her unhappy lot to fall; a degradation which was shared no less by clergy than by people—into which, indeed, the latter could not have fallen but for the worldly habits and shameless vices of their unworthy pastors. "The world is sick enough," indignantly cries Adrien Bourdoise, who was associated with St. Vincent in the laborious work of reformation; "but the clergy is not less so: frivolity, impurity, immodesty, are every where paramount. . . . . The majority of our priests stand with their arms folded; God is forced to raise up laymen — cutlers and haberdashers — to do the work of these lazy ecclesiastics. Seldom now-a-days do we meet with a man who is of good family and at the same time an instructed servant of God. Whence is it that God makes use of such laymen as M. Beaumais the draper, and M. Clement the cutler, as His instruments for the conversion of such numbers of heretics and bad Catholics in Paris, but that He finds not bachelors, licentiates, or doctors, filled with His Spirit, whom He can employ for the purpose? It is the heaviest reproach, the bitterest affront, He can offer the clergy of an age so devoid of humility. Long live the draper and the cutler! '*Non multi sapientes, non multi potentes, non multi nobiles.*'"*

The two remarkable men to whom M. Bourdoise here alludes seem to have been raised up in times of great irreligion to render extraordinary services to the Church. Jean Clement had been a Huguenot; after his conversion, he devoted himself to the teaching of Christian doctrine, and with such success that it is calculated in one year he made on an average no less than six converts a day. His practice was to take up a position near the church in which the Jesuit father Veron had just been preaching; there, gathering a crowd of auditors about him, he would explain in a plain and popular way the doctrines of the Church, and enforce the arguments of the learned but somewhat severe controversialist with a sweetness and an unction which few were able to resist. His extraordinary familiarity with the Sacred Scriptures—for it is recorded of him that he knew nearly the whole of the Bible in French by heart —gave him great influence with the Protestants, and especially with their preachers. He would first let them propose their doubts, and would then answer them with a readiness and a completeness truly marvellous in an uneducated man.

Beaumais also had been on the point of renouncing the faith in order to marry a Protestant, when, being unable to silence the reproaches of his conscience, he addressed himself to Jean Clement, who not only convinced him of the fatal character of the errors he was on the point of adopting, but induced him to join with him in teaching and defending the truth. He received by supernatural infusion a right understanding of the sense of the Scriptures and of the doctrines of the faith, and was considered to surpass in disputation the most famous doctors of the University of Paris. By the desire of M. Olier, who was anxious to obtain his co-

* 1 Cor. i. 26.

operation in reforming his parish, he took up his residence at St. Germain's; but he visited in turn all the towns of France which were most infected with Calvinism, and succeeded in bringing into the Church from four to five thousand heretics.

So secularised had the clergy become, that, in a Catholic country, where no excuse could be offered for such neglect of propriety, few wore any distinctive dress; they went about with moustaches and boots, like mere men of the world; nay, it would appear, in some instances, they did not take the trouble to put on their ecclesiastical attire even when performing some of the sacred offices of their calling. Thus it is related in the life of M. Bourdoise, who on principle always appeared publicly in his cassock, that going one day into the abbey-church of St. Denis, he saw a man seated in the sacristy with a coat and short cloak on, and booted and spurred, who was hearing the confession of a priest vested in alb and stole. He immediately went in search of the prior, and said to him, "My father, come here—come and see a cavalier confessing a priest!" The caustic rebuke had its effect; for the prior instantly gave peremptory orders to the sacristan to allow no such scandals for the future.

What wonder if the people were ignorant and immoral, when their teachers and guides had so little sense of decency or responsibility! A good prelate told Vincent one day that he was labouring to the best of his ability, with the assistance of his grand-vicars, for the improvement of his diocese, but with only poor success, on account of the great numbers of his clergy who were both ignorant and vicious, and on whom neither counsel nor example seemed to have any effect. "I tremble," he said, "when I think that my own diocese abounds in priests who are addicted to intemperance or who live incontinently, but who nevertheless approach the altar every day, although they are thus devoid of all vocation to the ecclesiastical state." Another bishop, writing to him, thus expressed himself: "With the exception of the canon theologian of my church, I do not know a single priest among all in my diocese who is competent to undertake any ecclesiastical charge. Judge, then, how great is our need of labourers."

The immediate causes of this deplorable state of things were, 1st, the absence of seminaries for the exclusive education of the clergy; and 2dly, the vicious system of patronage which then prevailed, and which, indeed, in spite of Vincent's reforms, was perpetuated through the influence of the secular power, till it helped to precipitate France into the vortex of the terrible revolution of 1789.

With few exceptions—so few as not to be worthy of being taken into account—there was not a diocese in France, notwithstanding the express injunctions of the Council of Trent, which had its ecclesiastical seminary, or which provided candidates for holy orders with a course of study and discipline preparatory to their entering on the ecclesiastical state. There were, it is true, schools in which dogmatics were taught; but moral theology was almost entirely neglected; and of individual training for all the practical duties of the Christian ministry there was virtually none. The future priests of the Church lived in the world, each following his own bent and inclinations, without restraint of any rule or superintendence of any kind, and without those special and most precious assistances which a community-life affords. There were no regular examinations, or spiritual retreats, or clerical conferences. Young men were admitted to the priesthood, and to the daily service of the altar, without any probation worthy of the name, and unfortified by those divine aids which human weakness requires for the discharge of so high and holy an office. St. Francis de Sales himself had failed in procuring a seminary for his diocese. M. Bourdoise once expressed his astonishment that he had not devoted himself to the formation of ecclesiastics. "I allow," replied the saint, with his characteristic humour and simplicity,—" indeed I am profoundly convinced that there is no need of the Church more pressing; but after toiling for more than seventeen years in endeavouring to form three priests to aid me in my ecclesiastical reforms, I have succeeded only in producing one and a half." However, towards the end of his life St. Francis had an intimate persuasion that Providence was about to raise up those who would accomplish what he had himself in vain laboured to effect.

But besides this negative evil,—the want of training and vocation for the priesthood,—there was the more active and positive one of the abuse of patronage, which was wholly in the hands of the crown and of the nobles, who filled the higher and more lucrative benefices with their scions and dependents, and in numerous instances with their illegitimate children. Many of the great abbeys, accordingly, were held by *laymen*, and even by *Protestants*; often, too, they were farmed out by the possessors, in order to raise ready money for their lavish expenditure. This corrupt and vicious system of patronage had invaded every portion of the clerical body, and acted most fatally in two ways; for, in the first place, the majority of the *cures*, or Church-livings, were in the gift of the abbeys, and were naturally supplied with ecclesiastics who were either the creatures of their patrons or persons of the same stamp as themselves; and in the second place, as their superiors were mere courtiers and men of the world, who simply appropriated to themselves the revenues of their office, and troubled themselves with none of its duties, so the religious and inferior clergy followed the example of those who were about them and over them, and became equally negligent and criminal.

The *Life of St. Vincent de Paul* furnishes two conspicuous instances of men thus unworthily promoted to most responsible offices in the Church. The first is that of Henry of Bourbon, Marquis of Verneuil, a natural son of Henry IV., who, although not even in holy orders, was Bishop of Metz, and at the same time held seven or eight rich benefices; being Abbé of St. Germain-des-Prés, Fécamp, Vauxsernai, Orchamps, St. Taurin d'Evreux, Bonport, Tiron, and Valaise. As Abbé of St. Germain's, he was possessed of extensive jurisdiction in the diocese of Paris, and might consequently have exercised a most powerful influence for good in that capital; but all the use he made of his great wealth and high position was to indulge in luxurious and dissolute living at court; and we shall find him, in the ensuing history, forsaking the people of his diocese in their terrible distress, and squandering at Paris those revenues which were derived from the patrimony of the Church and of the poor, and which, if rightly employed, might have rescued thousands from a frightful death, and from evils more to be dreaded than the worst temporal calamity. He ended by marrying.

The second instance is that of John Francis Paul de Gondi, the notorious Cardinal de Retz, who bore so prominent a part in the troubles of the Fronde. The bishopric (afterwards archbishopric) of Paris was for a whole century (1570 to 1670) a sort of appanage in his family, which was transmitted from uncle to nephew as though it had been an hereditary estate. His uncle, the first archbishop, whose coadjutor he was at the time of the struggle between the parliament and the court, was a man of irregular life, and allowed himself to be cajoled into favouring the Jansenists. As to the nephew, readers of history need not to be told, whatever view they may take of his political principles,* that he was a man whose ambition it was to be the head of a party in the state, and as unscrupulous in the means he employed to gain his ends as he was indefatigable

---

* According to his own account, his object was to restore the old moderate monarchy, such as existed in the days of St. Louis, which lay midway between positive democracy and that absolutism which had been, in a manner, founded by Richelieu, and was afterwards consolidated by Louis XIV.

in scheming and agitating for their attainment. Gifted with great natural powers, eloquent in speech, courageous in action, and able in the conduct of affairs, he was utterly destitute of all vocation to the ecclesiastical state, which he entered merely out of compliance with the wishes of his family. There is a painful interest in the account which this strange unprincipled man gives in his memoirs of the resolution he came to while in retreat at St. Lazarus (the house of St. Vincent's Congregation) before entering on a profession which he hated. "Being obliged to enter into orders, I retired to St. Lazarus, where I gave the exterior all the common appearances. My inward employment was to consider seriously and maturely in what manner I was to behave myself; in which I met with many difficulties. I found the archbishopric of Paris debased, as to the world, by my uncle's mean ways, and desolate, as to God, by his negligence and his incapacity. I foresaw infinite obstacles to the bringing it again upon a right footing; and I was not so blind but that I saw that the greatest and most insuperable came from myself. I was not ignorant of the necessity there is for a bishop to live regularly, and I was convinced that my uncle's disorderly and scandalous life made that necessity still greater and more indispensable in me. But at the same time, I found that it was not in my power to live in that manner; so that all the reasons which conscience or honour would suggest to me against an irregular life would prove but insignificant and weak. After six days' deliberation, I chose to act ill, designedly, which, as to God, is beyond comparison the most criminal, but which is without doubt the wisest as to the world. The reason is, that when you act in that manner, you always take some previous measures that will cover part of the ill action, so that you avoid besides the most dangerous sort of ridicule that persons of our profession can be exposed to, which is, the mixing preposterously sin with devotion. This was the holy disposition I was in when I left St. Lazarus. However, it was not bad in every respect; for I had fully resolved to discharge exactly all the outward duties of my profession, and to take as much care of other people's souls as I took little of my own."*

Accordingly, he took pains to conceal his licentiousness from both clergy and people, and was so decorous and guarded in his outward conduct, that the most active and learned priests of the diocese were anxious to see him promoted to be his uncle's coadjutor. To serve his political and private ends, as he himself avows, he occasionally attended, when in orders, the spiritual conferences instituted by St. Vincent; he studied theology, preached, disputed with heretics, and was liberal in almsgiving. Yet all this time, as his memoirs show, he was an artful political intriguer and an habitual debauchee. Not that he affected " godliness,"—he was too honest or too careless for that; nor that in his heart he ridiculed devotion,—on the contrary, evil-liver as he was, he seems to have entertained a real admiration for virtue and piety. But he had deliberately chosen his portion—the honours of the world, and as much of its pleasures as was compatible with the attainment of credit and power. To do him justice, he appears to have had some scruples as to degrading the priestly character in the eyes of the multitude, and thus diminishing the influence of religion and morality. This, indeed, seems to have been the one redeeming point in his character: deliberately choosing evil, he never at least deceived himself into thinking that he was other than he was, nor ceased to do homage to virtue, though he had not the will to follow it. He boasts that St. Vincent, whose pupil he had been, said of him at the beginning of his career, that though he was then devoid of all piety, he was not far from the kingdom of God. Such words from the lips of such a man are prophetic; and that towards the end of his life he sincerely repented, and became " a model of gravity, piety,

* "Memoirs of the Cardinal de Retz, written by himself" (Evans's translation), vol. i. p. 56-57.

disinterestedness, and beneficence," may be attributed, under the grace of God, to the advantage he had derived from the instructions and example of his saintly preceptor, and—may we not with certainty add?—his prayers and his merits.*

Strange that under the rule of such an archbishop, such a coadjutor—of all men, as he says of himself, perhaps the least ecclesiastical—and such an Abbé of St. Germain, was to commence a most real, thorough, and, in its measure, lasting reformation of the clergy, and, through them, of the population, not of Paris alone, but of France; and this by means of a poor shepherd-lad, who did his utmost to keep himself and his virtues out of the sight of men, and especially of those who in any way could forward his temporal interests! Strange in the eyes of the world; but not strange, though wonderful, to those who know that God loves to exalt the humble, and to use things that are weak to the confusion of the strong.

The circumstances under which Vincent de Paul made his first act of self-dedication to God,—an act which, speaking humanly, was the turning-point in his life, and the commencement of his apostolic career,—are as remarkable in themselves as they are characteristic of the man. In the household of Queen Margaret of Valois, first consort of Henry IV., at the time that Vincent was her chaplain, lived a certain divine who had much zeal for religion and had engaged successfully in controversy with heretics and infidels. This man, for some end known only to God, was assailed with violent temptations against the faith, which led him to the verge of despair. No sooner did he attempt

* Neither ought we to forget the Count and Countess de Joigny, the Cardinal's pious parents, and Vincent's early patrons and joint-founders with him of the Congregation of the Priests of the Mission. The Count, on his wife's death, entered the French Oratory, where he died. Cardinal de Retz eventually resigned two abbeys he held, and also his archbishopric; and would have laid aside the purple, but that Pope Clement X. would not consent to his doing so.

to say Mass, recite his office, or so much as begin a *Pater noster*, than all the powers of hell seemed to be let loose against him. Vincent's advice to him was, that whenever he was thus tempted he should make a simple act of faith, by inclining his head, or raising a finger in the direction of Rome or of some neighbouring church. The divine fell ill, and his temptations grew stronger. Vincent, full of fear lest his friend should yield to the assaults of the enemy, ceased not to implore the divine mercy in his behalf; he offered himself to God in the sufferer's stead, to undergo the same interior trials, or any other chastisement His justice might be pleased to lay upon him. The sacrifice was accepted to its full extent; the priest recovered his peace of mind; but the temptation from which he was freed was transferred to his generous deliverer. Terrible was the conflict; the more Vincent redoubled his prayers and mortifications, the fiercer grew the assaults of the tempter; but Vincent lost not courage, and kept his heart fixed on God. At length he did two things: he committed his confession of faith to writing, and placed it on his breast; then, making a general disavowal of all thoughts against faith, he entered into a solemn compact with our Lord, that whenever he but touched the spot where the paper lay, the act should be taken as a renewal of his profession of faith and a renunciation of the doubts suggested to him, although no word should pass his lips. He thus frustrated all the designs of the adversary. The second remedy he adopted was, to do the very contrary of that to which he was tempted, and to devote himself more than ever to honouring Jesus Christ in the persons of His suffering members. Four years had passed in this hard battle, when he was moved to make a firm and inviolable resolution, for the greater honour of Jesus and to imitate Him more perfectly, to give himself up, out of pure and simple love of Him, for the rest of his life wholly to the service of the poor. Hardly had he formed this resolution when the suggestions of the evil one entirely ceased, and his soul was filled with such abundant light, that he seemed not so much to believe, as to *see* the truths of faith.

Vincent had thought but to be the servant of the poor; but God had chosen him to be the teacher of the wise and the counsellor of princes. From being the missioner of ignorant country-people, he was to become the reformer of the clergy of France and the regenerator of his country. We shall find him instituting spiritual retreats and exercises for such as were about to enter holy orders; weekly conferences, in which the clergy conferred together on matters connected with the ecclesiastical state, its virtues and its duties; a seminary, in which the newly ordained, or such as were preparing for ordination, might "pass one or two years in studying the higher branches of theology, the ritual of the Church, the administration of the Sacraments, catechising, and preaching;" and lastly, a little seminary, in which youths might, from an early age, be trained for the service of the altar.* "This last institution," to quote again the words of his biographer, "completed the whole work; and thus, from first to last, from childhood till death, Vincent had provided the clergy of his diocese with spiritual nurture. The boy who entered the seminary of St. Charles might in due time pass to that of the Bons Enfans to complete his clerical studies; the Priory of St. Lazarus received him at the end of his course for his solemn retreat before ordination; and when he had entered upon the duties of his state the same doors were opened weekly to admit him to the spiritual conferences, which strengthened and encouraged him in his arduous duties; while once a year he was called again into a longer retreat, that he might take account of his spiritual state and prepare for the end."†

---

* "Vincent de Paul," says Rohrbacher (vol. xxv. p. 315), "was the first in France, perhaps in the whole world, to carry into effect the intentions of the Council of Trent, in the foundation both of a larger and a smaller seminary."

† Life, pp. 86, 87.

All this time similar institutions were springing up in other parts of France; for Vincent had most noble and saintly emulators, or rather fellow-labourers, in the same great field of ecclesiastical reform, working independently, yet like members of one united confraternity, in the service of the Church. Among the celebrated men of exalted virtue and heroic lives who frequented the Tuesday conferences of St. Lazarus were Adrien Bourdoise (to whom allusion has been made), so zealous in the cause of ecclesiastical reform, and founder of the Seminary of St. Nicholas-du-Chardonnet; Claude Bernard, self-styled, in humility, the "poor priest," one of the most powerful preachers, as he was certainly one of the most original men of his day, the brilliancy of whose wit, which attracted to him all that was great and good in Paris, was equalled only by his burning charity and love for souls,—he was founder of the Seminary of the Trente-Trois, so called from the thirty-three years of our Saviour's life on earth; Jean Jacques Olier, the most saint-like, as he has been called, of uncanonised men, reformer *par excellence* of the secular clergy, and founder of the Seminary and Congregation of St. Sulpice; Jean Duval, Bishop of Babylon, founder of the House and Congregation of the Foreign Missions; the celebrated Bossuet, Bishop of Meaux, who himself, when one of the clergy of Metz, assisted at a mission given in that place by Vincent de Paul. It is thus that the last spoke of the Saint and of his conferences and retreats in a letter addressed to Pope Clement XI.: "When we were promoted to the priesthood, it was to Vincent that we owed the preparation which we made; and it was under his direction and animated by his counsels that from time to time we went through the spiritual retreats which he had instituted; we had also the happiness of being associated with that company of virtuous ecclesiastics who assembled every week to confer together on the things of God. Vincent was the author and the very life and soul of those assemblies. He never opened his lips but we all listened to him with an insatiable avidity, and felt in our inmost heart that Vincent was one of those men of whom the Apostle said, 'If any man speak, let him speak as the words of God. If any man minister, let him do it as of the power which God administereth.'" Nor, amongst those who prepared the way for the establishment of seminaries and reform of the clergy, or assisted in giving to France a learned and virtuous priesthood, must we omit to mention the great Oratorians, Cardinal de Bérulle and F. de Condren; the Jesuits, Hayneuve and St. Jure; and the Benedictines, Tarisse and Bataille.

But Vincent laboured not only to infuse fresh health and vigour into the ecclesiastical body, but to stem the tide of corruption which poisoned its very life-springs. We shall find this humble priest called on by the supreme power in the state to recommend and in effect to nominate the bishops and prelates of France; and this, not with the bare concurrence, but at the earnest solicitations of one whom the reader of secular history knows only as the stern, impassive, iron-handed politician, Cardinal Richelieu. As Catholics, as those who believe that nothing, not national aggrandisement, or pre-eminence, or independence, can outweigh or is so much as worthy of being named in comparison with the interests of the faith of Christ and the Church which He founded, we must unreservedly condemn the policy which Richelieu pursued. That policy was a policy of worldly expediency. He, a prince of Holy Church, leagued himself for reasons of state with the implacable enemies of the faith; "with utter indifference to the vital interests of religion transferring the government of the Valteline, which was Catholic, from Spain to the Protestant Grisons; exciting the Protestant princes of Germany to carry devastation into the Catholic countries of the south, and seeking every occasion to strengthen their force."* First and foremost in his mind stood France,

* *Mores Catholici*, b. v. c. 10. That shrewd observer, Cardinal de Retz, says of him: "His stock of religion was sufficient for this world. He was led to do good, either by his own good

its temporal glory and material prosperity; and afterwards came "the kingdom of God and His justice." Yet, when the interests of religion did not interfere with the interests, or what he regarded as the interests, of the state, or appeared coincident therewith, he was as zealous in promoting them as he was clear-sighted in discerning the measures to be adopted and the men he could rely upon for their execution. As early as the year 1614, when, being Bishop of Luçon, he was deputy for Poitou, he had harangued the States General on the subject of ecclesiastical reform, with especial reference to the abuse of patronage; and had called upon the king, in the strongest and most moving terms, to apply the only effectual remedy to the evil, by receiving and executing the decrees of the Council of Trent. With the powerful help of this great minister, Vincent was enabled to effect most salutary and important changes; and after Richelieu's death his position as a member of the Council of Conscience, in which capacity he possessed a sort of veto on all appointments to the highest offices in the Church, gave him extraordinary facilities in carrying the needed reforms into places where corruption had hitherto reigned supreme.

Not that Vincent was able to penetrate altogether to the root of the evil; for that root lay deeply imbedded in the heart of that whole system of government in respect to the Church which had become nationalised in France—a system characterised by one dominant idea, jealousy of the Holy See, which is of the very spirit of schism; for it is nothing less than a contemptuous and undutiful revolt against the source of all ecclesiastical jurisdiction and authority, in other words, the supremacy of Him to whom all power has been given, in the person of His earthly Vicar. This emphatically was the spring and primary cause of the corruptions that prevailed in the clergy and in society.

sense or by his inclination, whenever his interest did not lead him a contrary way, in which case he had a perfect knowledge of the ill he did."

Rome was made as light of, and kept as much at a distance, as was compatible with a profession on the part of the state of communion with the Apostolic See; hence the absorption by the crown and the nobles of all the patronage of the Church, so that, as it has been truly and forcibly said, "the Holy See ceased to be primarily responsible for the way in which it was dispensed."* This is not the place to do more than indicate the real source of the evils which afflicted and degraded the Church of France; the mischief lay too deep for reform, it needed a revolution—and such a revolution!—or rather revolution upon revolution, to expel the virus, and restore a body so organically diseased to health and soundness. What wonder, then, if even a Vincent de Paul, and the saints and saintly men who were his fellow-labourers, were unable to effect more than a partial and incomplete cure? Yet the change he wrought was so great and so striking, that, in comparison with what had been the state of things at the commencement of his labours, it might justly be called a restoration to life; and a venerable prelate could say boldly in the face of the Saint's contemporaries, "To Vincent de Paul the clergy of France owe their splendour and renown."

Such is the unfailing vigour, the self-recuperative power, of every living portion of the Church Catholic, even in times of the greatest depravity. It is able to produce saints; and not alone those rare and extraordinary creations of Divine grace, but crowds of holy men and holy women, poor in spirit, clean of heart, and filled with the love of God, any one of whom would be regarded as a marvel and a prodigy outside the Church. The France of St. Vincent's days abounded in such; not Paris alone, but each provincial town had those within it who were not merely good and religious

* *Dublin Review*, No. lxxii., article "Jansenism, Gallicanism, and Jacobinism," to which the reader is referred for an able account of the causes of the evils under which the Church of France laboured.

people, but whom a cold and scoffing world would call pious enthusiasts—men and women who really preferred God before all things else, and were devoted to His service, and to the service of the poor and the afflicted simply for His sake. So that where sin abounded, grace did still more abound; and grievous as were the scandals caused by an unfaithful clergy and a dissolute nobility, the pure lives of these true Catholics, and their deeds of holy heroism, shed a glorious lustre over the gloomy days in which they lived.

Nor was it among the higher and more educated classes alone that these bright examples were to be found. The ranks of the people yielded many a devout child of Holy Church, and many an ardent reformer; some from the first open and avowed, others known only to God, until He was pleased to make their virtues and labours public in spite of themselves. Of the former were Clement the cutler, and Beaumais the draper (of whom mention has been made), and Claude Leglay, whom the great archdeacon of Evreux, Boudon, calls "the good Lorrain," and who, M. Olier says, had the very spirit of Elias, and a heart all on fire and consumed with the love of God. Of the latter was Mary de Gournay. Her life, and indeed the very existence of such a person at such a time, furnishes so remarkable a testimony to that world of sanctity which lay hidden beneath the surface of society in France, that it deserves a passing notice. She was the wife of a tavern-keeper in Paris; and although possessed of a moderate competency, such was her love of poverty and of the poor, that her dress was ever of the meanest, and her food consisted only of scraps and morsels which others would have rejected. Her humility and contempt of herself corresponded with the austerity of her life. Her one great object was to imitate the blessed Mother of God, and in all things to conform her interior dispositions to those with which that incomparable Virgin performed the most ordinary action. In her fear of attracting the esteem of others, she carefully avoided every thing which might gain her the reputation of being a person of piety; and during the twenty years she pursued her avocation, amidst the constant bustle and distraction of a place of public entertainment, she allowed nothing to appear which could betray her extraordinary sanctity and entire union with God. Not but that by some simple timely word she arrested many a sinner in his headlong course, and drew many a guilty soul to repentance; still there was nothing about her to distinguish her from a thousand others of her class. At her husband's death, she chose for herself the worst room in the house, and one too that, from its situation, was never free from noise, to which she was naturally most averse; but there she made a solitude to herself as perfect as though it had been a cave in a desert. She gave herself up to Divine contemplation; the only desire of her heart being that she might speedily behold face to face Him whom her soul loved. The Most Holy Eucharist was to her as meat and drink; so that she sometimes passed whole days without any other nourishment.

This woman, so humble and obscure, and (at least for many years of her life) to all outward appearance devoted to a most unspiritual, and, as some might even think, disreputable calling, was possessed with one longing desire—the reformation of the clergy. For this she never ceased making most earnest supplication to God; for this she offered all her mortifications and good works. M. Olier, then a youth of twenty years, was one day returning with his companions from a fair at which they had been diverting themselves, when a poor woman, as if her heart was wrung with sorrow, said to them, "Ah, sirs, I have long prayed for your conversion, and I hope God will still hear my prayers!" It was Mary de Gournay. At her words M. Olier felt himself moved to break with the world and give himself up to God. The Church knows the result. From that moment dates the conversion of the founder of St. Sulpice. His first act was to put himself under the direction

of St. Vincent, who prepared him for holy orders, and
employed him on his country missions; but the person
who of all others most contributed to the establishment of his first seminary was this despised *cabaretière*
— the mistress of a public-house! Her virtues and
her piety were no longer to be hidden under a bushel.
"This woman of low extraction," writes M. Olier, "and
of a condition in life which it is almost a disgrace to
name, is become the adviser of persons the most illustrious by birth and rank, and the guide of souls the
most exalted in virtue. Even princesses have recourse
to her counsels, and recommend themselves and their
undertakings to her prayers. The Duchess of Orleans,
the Princess of Condé, the Duchesses d'Aiguillon and
d'Elbeuf, the Marchioness de la Châtre, and many
others, count it an honour to visit her; indeed, I have
known a lady of the highest rank afraid of going into
her presence, such was the veneration she had for her
character. Souls the most advanced in the ways of
perfection seek lessons of guidance from her lips; men
of the most apostolic spirit go to consult her before
entering on any enterprise which they have in contemplation. F. Eudes, that famous preacher, the
wonder of the age; F. de Condren, Superior of the
Oratory; Mdlle. de Manse, raised up by God to the
aid of the infant Church of Canada; M. le Royer de la
Dauversière, to whom that Church may be said to owe
its first establishment; M. du Coudray, devoted to the
missions of the Levant and the defence of Christendom
against the Turks; Dom Jacques, the Carthusian, the
bold rebuker of vice in the wealthy and the powerful;—when these, and so many others of the most
zealous servants of God who at this day adorn the
Church of France, are to be seen seeking counsel of
this wise and holy woman, we might think we beheld
the 'Virgin most prudent' once more directing the
Church of her Divine Son, and guiding His Apostles
after His ascension into heaven. She has but to speak,
and at a word all that she asks or wishes is done; and

that without any of the exterior address or air and manner of command by which such influence is usually exerted."*

They who rail at the wickedness and shamelessness of the age, and make it a reproach to the Church of France that such vices and abuses prevailed around her and within her, forget or are ignorant of all this; they choose to ignore the fact that this Church, so corrupt and worldly as they deem her, nevertheless produced those three magnificent Saints,—a Francis de Sales, a Jane Frances de Chantal, and a Vincent de Paul, and that contemporaneously. If England,† within a term of three hundred years, can boast of a single Howard, how great is the glory of France, and of the Church of France, which in a single generation gave birth to some three hundred such as he, and more than he! Nothing, indeed, is more remarkable in the annals of that Church and country than the array of devoted men and women, and the multitude of noble institutions, both religious and charitable, which signalised an age notorious only in secular history for selfishness, luxury, profligacy, and general hollowness. The present biography bears ample testimony to the truth of this assertion: it is but the narrative of what one man accomplished; and, as has already been said, kindred works, more or less connected with St. Vincent's labours, were going forward at the same time in all parts of France. What an evidence is here of the immense amount of goodness that existed in closest juxtaposition with the worst depravity! Such works, so numerous and so multifarious, could not have been begun or carried on by the few who

---

* Abridged from the "Life of M. Olier."

† Not the "Church of England," for Howard was an Independent: indeed his acts of self-devotion were the product of his own generous and God-loving heart, and cannot be referred to any religious sect or party. They were the acts of an individual; and as they originated with himself, so they terminated with himself: he founded no institution, he left no successors.

originated them, but by the co-operation of a multitude of auxiliaries; and these again must have found, as in fact they did find, willing subjects whereon to exercise their mission, and who responded to, or at least succumbed before, the influences brought to bear upon them. The people of France were sincerely, cordially Catholic, and had all the moral and religious susceptibilities, and all the capacity of vividly realising supernatural truths, which characterise those who possess the gift of faith. Say that the clergy were supine and vicious, that society was depraved and corrupt; yet it is the fact that that same clergy obeyed the call of the preachers of penance, and submitted to the discipline prescribed by their reformers; and that the people by thousands recognised the voice of their true pastors, and with tears of genuine contrition confessed their sins and amended their lives. And where is the Church not in communion with the See of Peter, in which such a revival has been begun and effectuated, not by eccentric and extraordinary influences as from without, but by the regularly organised efforts of its own proper pastors, and by the authority and under the direction of its own bishops and prelates?—a true and solid reformation, not a barren and faithless compromise on some lower platform of expediency; not a patching up and hiding of sores for which no cure could be found, or the remedies for which men would not tolerate; but a real restoration, and a vigorous enforcement of ecclesiastical discipline; a return and a rising again to the highest and holiest standard of religious practice.

The Archbishop of Paris, weak man as he was, and vain-glorious, and even scandalous in his private life, willingly helped on the movement. We shall find him bestowing on Vincent de Paul the College des Bons Enfans as a residence for his Congregation, and requiring from every candidate for ordination in his diocese a ten days' retreat under the Saint's direction. His nephew, De Retz, was no sooner appointed his coadjutor, than he, on his part, undertook to examine into the sufficiency of all the priests under his jurisdiction, erecting for that purpose three tribunals, composed of canons, curés, and religious, who were to make a threefold division; 1st, of priests who were adequately proficient in the learning and knowledge necessary for their state; 2dly, of those who were insufficiently instructed, but were capable of learning; 3dly, of those who were neither instructed nor capable. The first were allowed to continue the exercise of their functions; the second received such instruction as they needed; while the third were only taught to live piously. For this great object he relates that considerable sums were brought to him from all parts, and there was not a pious man whose purse was not liberally opened. At the same time his private charities were great, and now, whatever might have been the case before his elevation, from no love of ostentation; on the contrary, he strove to conceal them, and his liberality sprang, as he says, from no other motive than his natural inclination, and the single view of what might justly be expected from him. Not that he had repented of his immoralities, or that his secret life was more in accordance with the Divine rule; but he knew what was due to his episcopal character, and, outwardly at least, desired to conform to the obligations of his state. Even Mazarin, for all his contempt of religion, was carried along by a movement which he could not resist, though he attempted to thwart it by appearing to control it, and was Vincent's reluctant ally in his work of reformation. The inner life and the outward behest of the Church proved too strong for such men; and they either surrendered themselves voluntarily to the tide of improvement, or struggled impotently, and were borne on against their will.

So true it is, that in days the most evil, and in despite of individual delinquency and unfaithfulness on the part of those in authority, the Church, corporately and collectively, ever bears witness against the world: the quality of her teaching is not strained. her standard of morality is not lowered, the instincts of her children are not blunted; public opinion within her pale ever approves and upholds the holiest rule, the severest restraints; her priests are preachers of justice, her prelates are zealous for the Divine law and the discipline of a holy life; saints are her natural product, and their labours and successes are her own.

E. H. T.

CONTENTS.

CHAP.		PAGE
I.	Birth, youth, and college life	1
II.	Vincent in slavery	8
III.	First visit to Paris	15
IV.	Vincent in the family of De Gondi	20
V.	Vincent among the galley-slaves	31
VI.	Vincent at Mâcon	34
VII.	Vincent and St. Jane Frances de Chantal	40
VIII.	The Countess de Joigny and the New Order	46
IX.	The College des Bons Enfans	53
X.	The Priory of St. Lazarus	68
XI.	Institutions for the clergy	77
XII.	Madame Le Gras	89
XIII.	The Sisters of Charity	94
XIV.	The Hôtel-Dieu	101
XV.	The Foundling Hospital	108
XVI.	Convicts, idiots, and reprobates	114
XVII.	Lorraine—its sufferings and its succours	121
XVIII.	Vincent in office	140
XIX.	Vincent and Jansenism	152
XX.	The foreign missions	162
XXI.	Missions in Ireland	177
XXII.	Vincent's tour of visitation and succour of Picardy	186
XXIII.	The Hospital of the Name of Jesus, and the General Hospital	196
XXIV.	Death and Canonisation of Vincent de Paul	203

LIFE OF ST. VINCENT DE PAUL.

Life of St. Vincent de Paul.

CHAPTER I.
BIRTH, YOUTH, AND COLLEGE LIFE.

WE should obtain a very partial and inadequate idea of the social and religious state of France in the first half of the seventeenth century, were we to overlook or to undervalue the part that was played during that eventful period by the truly great man, a sketch of whose life and labours is here presented to the reader. For if, on the one hand, it be true that we cannot separate Vincent de Paul from the world around him without depriving him of half his glory, and his actions of much of their significance and interest, equally true is it, on the other, that we should make ourselves but imperfectly acquainted with the characteristics of the age in which he lived, and its bearing on succeeding times, if we put out of sight, or excluded from our consideration, the works that were achieved, and the institutions that were founded, by one of the most energetic reformers, as well as most distinguished apostles of charity, whom mankind has ever seen. Humble and retiring as he was by natural disposition, as well as by divine grace, he yet exercised an influence upon his country which produced wonderful effects in his own day, and which, far from passing away with his earthly life, has continued to grow and augment, until, in the present age, it makes itself felt beyond the confines of France, and knows no limit but such as bounds humanity itself.

In the eye of the historian, indeed, Vincent de Paul was only a simple priest, who contented himself with doing his work in a quiet, unobtrusive way, and who, making no great noise in the world, scarcely attracted the attention of his contemporaries, and gained no place in the pages of his country's annals. True he could reckon a cardinal and more than one crowned head among his truest friends; and in times of need he could fill, with more than ordinary success, the responsible office of councillor and adviser to a queen regent; but these, it may be said, were the exception and not the rule of his life. Nevertheless, Vincent de Paul was one of those real heroes whose influence upon their contemporaries is far greater than that of men whose names are familiar to all. They originate movements in which others acquire renown; they sow the seeds, while others reap the harvest; they change, it may be, the very habits and manners of a nation: and yet history is silent as to their course, and neglects to recognise their power.

So was it with Vincent de Paul. Many a student of French history may never have met with his name, and yet it may be questioned whether any one man has done more to benefit his country than this poor single-hearted priest. How few who have read of those fierce civil wars which devastated France for more than a century and a half, have ever thought of Vincent de Paul as one of the great and influential characters in those times of agitation and peril! Names there are, familiar to us as household words, which rise almost unconsciously to our lips when the deeds of those dark days are mentioned; yet what place does this great Saint occupy in the list? Guise, Coligny, Condé, Montmorency, Henry of Navarre, Mary of Medicis, Richelieu, and Mazarin,—who is not acquainted with these, and a host of others, who fill the page of history and stand out so prominently in those terrible pictures which fix themselves indelibly upon the memory? Yet is there one as great and as influential as any of them, of whom the general reader knows literally nothing.

Could we forget the incessant antagonism of the Church and the world, we might almost wonder that, for the mere sake of relief and artistic contrast, the secular historian should not sometimes notice such men as Vincent de Paul. Who has not grown wearied with the never-ending scenes of intrigue and bloodshed which form the staple of what is commonly called history? who has not laid down with aching heart the volume which, however skilfully it may have set forth the crimes of former days, fatigues by the weight of guilt and injustice which it so faithfully records? who has not longed for the appearance of some new personages who, like Vincent, might play an angel's part in the very worst of these sad times, and show that a merciful Providence has never ceased to raise up powerful instruments to alleviate the suffering which then most calls for help; and who, when hearts are coldest and religion seems well nigh banished from the land, bear about in their own pure souls the undying fire of love, and kindle on all sides the expiring embers into a genial flame? Surely characters like these are intended as the consolation of history; they are as bright stars to lighten at night, as sweet tokens of a divine presence in the midst of sin and infidelity, as green spots upon which the wearied may rest in traversing that dreary wilderness which men's passions have made of the world's chronicles.

In the village of Pouy, near Dax in Gascony, there lived, in the latter part of the sixteenth century, a poor villager named John de Paul, who struggled hard to support his wife and six children upon the produce of the little piece of land which his family helped him to cultivate. He was a simple open-hearted peasant; one who lived in the fear and love of God, and who in his own plain way trained up his children in the same pious course. His wife, Bertranda de Moras, was the fitting partner of such a man; and thus they lived not only without reproach, but with edification to their neighbours. The village contained a chapel dedicated to the Mother of God, under the name of *Our Lady of Buglose*, which was much frequented by the people of those parts as a place of pilgrimage.

Among the children of this humble family was one, the fourth, born in 1576, whose fervent piety and precocious ability attracted the especial attention of his parents. He laboured in the fields with the others; he shared in the watching of the sheep and swine; yet he was unlike those about him. The power of Mary was there where her name was so especially honoured, and the heart of the youthful Vincent seemed to expand beneath its influence, and to have capacity to receive it in its fulness. Nor did his intellect lag behind his affections. The poor shepherd boy, in his silent wanderings in the sandy *Landes*, communed with God and his own heart; divine grace strengthening what it had first implanted, the child grew in favour with God and man, like the Divine Infant whose in an especial manner he was, and whom he was to serve so faithfully in a long life.

The piety and genius of the young Vincent were not unmarked by his father, who plainly saw that he was destined for some higher station than that which the family occupied; and what naturally suggested itself to his pious mind but that which is the highest to which a Christian can aspire? "He must be a priest," said the poor peasant. Nor did the position appear beyond his reach; for it seems there was a neighbouring family in no better circumstances than his own which had given a priest to Holy Church, who had since become the prior of an adjacent convent, and who failed not to repay the past sacrifices of his family by doing much to advance his own brothers. Perhaps this latter circumstance was not without its influence upon John de Paul when he determined to educate his pious child, and worldly prudence might have its share in strengthening him for the sacrifice such a determination required. But man proposes, and God disposes. The sacrifice was made; the boy in due time became a priest; but in no earthly respect did his family profit thereby, as the event showed. Years afterwards, when Vincent was living in Paris, a priest from his native place visited him to urge him to do something for his relations, who were as poor as ever. He only replied: "Do they not live as of old, honestly and contentedly, by their labour, in the state in which God placed them?" And then he went on to show, from the example of this very prior, how little the families of priests profit by what they gain from the Church; and how, as in this particular case, it too often happens, that wealth thus obtained brings with it a curse rather than a blessing. Those who enrich themselves with the portion of the poor, God sooner or later deprives of such ill-gotten gain. There is little danger of this action being misunderstood; Vincent's heart was too tender, his affections too warm, for any to accuse him of coldness and apathy. When his own personal interests alone stood in the way of his liberality, the stream of charity flowed on unchecked, as is well illustrated by a circumstance which occurred when he was about twelve years of age. He had managed to save up from time to time as much as thirty sous,—a large sum for one so young, and in a place where money was so scarce,—when one day he met a poor man in such great distress that his heart was fairly overcome, and he gave him the whole of his little treasure.

When his father had determined to educate Vincent for the priesthood, the question arose as to the cheapest way of doing so, for his narrow means could at best but furnish little; he therefore sent him to the Franciscan friars at Dax, who agreed to receive him for the small pension of sixty livres, about six pounds a-year. It was in 1588 that he began his studies with the rudiments of Latin; and in four years he had made such progress, that M. Commet, a lawyer in the town, upon the recommendation of the father-guardian of the convent, received him into his house as tutor to his children. This at once relieved John de Paul from the burden of his son's support, and enabled Vincent, with a quiet mind and without any misgivings on that head, to pursue his own studies while he formed the characters of his little pupils. For five years he continued in this position, when M. Commet felt it his duty to part with one whom he loved as a son, and who had edified his whole family by his piety. He saw that Vincent was called to a holier state and to a higher sphere than that which he then occupied; and with an aching heart and with many tears he sent the youthful scholar to the university of Toulouse, having first procured for him minor orders at Dax. This was in 1596, when Vincent was twenty years of age. Vincent never again saw his native province. His parents sent him their blessing, and sold two of their oxen to provide him with the means for his journey.

He continued his studies at Toulouse for seven years; but during that interval he visited Spain, and remained for some time at the university of Saragossa.

He was made subdeacon on the 27th of February 1598, and deacon on the 29th of December of the same year; and on September 23d, 1600, he was promoted to the priesthood. When and where he said his first Mass is not known; all that could ever be learned from him on the subject was, that he was so impressed with the majesty of the divine action, and so overwhelmed with a sense of his own utter unworthiness to offer such a tremendous sacrifice, that he had not courage enough to celebrate publicly, and that, therefore, he chose a retired chapel, when none were present but a server and a priest to direct him.

As soon as he was ordained, the Vicar-general of Dax (the bishopric being at that time vacant) appointed him to the parish of Tilh, as much through regard for Vincent himself as on account of his old friend M. de Commet, who solicited that preferment for him. But, fortunately for the young priest, a competitor arose, who disputed the appointment and appealed to Rome; and Vincent, being unwilling to enter into a contest, gave up his claim, and thus was enabled to continue the studies which he loved so much.

Vincent might have claimed a maintenance from his family; for his father had died some two years before, and in his will had left our Saint enough for this purpose; but he determined to burden his family no further, and accepted a tutorship which was offered to him at Buset, about twelve miles from Toulouse. Here several of the neighbouring gentry sent their sons to board with him, and some came also from Toulouse,— as he told his mother in a letter he wrote about this time. His success with his pupils, and the great attachment they formed for him, enabled him shortly afterwards to return to Toulouse and to take them with him, and thus was he enabled to continue his theological studies. It was not until after his death that it was known how long and how successfully he had studied in this university. He always spoke of himself as a poor scholar who had gone through a four-years' course, which was true enough, as we have seen that at the end of that course he left Toulouse; but in his humility and desire to conceal the honours he had gained, he said nothing of his subsequent return, nor of the degree of bachelor of divinity which he gained in 1604, nor of the other distinctions which he received there. It required a search in the archives of the university to find the official documents which certify to these honours, which the Saint so carefully concealed.

CHAPTER II.

VINCENT IN SLAVERY.

During the time that Vincent remained at Toulouse, he continued to gain the esteem of all who came in contact with him. The number of his pupils increased, and a fair prospect of success presented itself. But a higher and more important position was opening before him. For it appears that he had been given to understand that the powerful Duke d'Epernon would use his great influence to obtain a bishopric for the favourite tutor of two of his near relations. Such were his prospects, when an event occurred which frustrated all these plans, and gave a new turn to his quiet and studious life. The providence of God designed to try him before giving him his great work; he must pass, like so many other saints, through the furnace of affliction, that the precious metal of his soul might be tempered for the task about to be committed to him.

Business of importance called him from Toulouse to Bourdeaux. He made the journey, and was on his return to Toulouse, when he learned that one of his friends had died during his absence, and left him heir to a considerable sum of money. One of the debtors of this friend had run away to Marseilles to avoid paying what he owed, although he had plenty of means of so doing. Vincent therefore went to Marseilles, and agreed to accept a sum of three hundred crowns in payment of this debt. It was in July 1605 that he arranged this affair; and he was on the point of returning to Toulouse by land, when a fellow-traveller persuaded him to go by water to Narbonne; an arrangement to which he willingly consented, as it was a fair season and promised a shorter journey. During this voyage he was captured by some African pirates, and carried prisoner to Tunis. A letter has been preserved, in which he relates the whole matter to one of his earliest pupils, the son of his old patron M. de Commet.

"I set out," he says, "for Narbonne by water, that I might arrive there the sooner and spend less money; or, I should rather say, that I might never arrive there at all, and that I might lose all I possessed. The wind was so favourable, that we should have made the voyage to Narbonne in a single day, though it was a distance of 150 miles, had not God permitted three Turkish brigantines (which were coasting along the gulf of Lyons, to waylay the vessels that sailed from Beaucaire, where there is one of the best markets in Christendom) to attack and board us so fiercely, that two or three of our party were killed, and all the rest wounded, and I received a wound from an arrow which I shall remember for the rest of my life; so we were obliged to surrender to these pirates. The first effect of their rage was the murder of our pilot, whom they hacked to pieces, in revenge for the loss of one of their chiefs, and of four or five galley-slaves, whom our men had killed; after this they cast us all into chains, and having dressed us in scant clothing, they continued their course of pillage on other vessels, but always gave liberty to those who submitted without opposition to their depredations. At length, after seven or eight days, they directed their vessel, laden with merchandise, towards Barbary,—that den and hiding-place of the Grand Turk's shameless thieves. When we arrived there, we were exposed for sale, with a formal declaration of our capture, which set forth that we were taken in a Spanish vessel; because, but for this falsehood, we should have been liberated by the consul whom our king has placed there to protect the interests of the French. They set about our sale in this way: first they stripped us; then they gave each of us a pair of drawers, a linen coat, and a cap; thus equipped, they marched us through the city of Tunis, whither they went expressly to sell us. After taking us round the city five or six times, with chains about our necks, they brought us back to the boat, that the merchants might see who could feed well, and who could not, and that our wounds were not mortal. This done, they led us back to the market-place, where the merchants came and examined us as they do horses and cattle at a fair; making us open our mouths and show our teeth, pinching our sides and probing our wounds, and making us walk, trot, and run, lift burdens and wrestle, to show our strength, besides a thousand other brutalities.

"I was sold to a fisherman, who was soon constrained to get rid of me; for nothing disagrees with me like the sea. He sold me to an old chemist, a mighty extractor of quintessences, a humane and easy personage, who, as he told me, had toiled for fifty years in search of the philosopher's stone. He loved me greatly, and took pleasure in talking with me about alchemy, and still more about his law; to which he used every effort to attract me, promising me all his riches and all his knowledge. God worked in me all along a belief that I should gain my liberty through the assiduous prayers which I offered to Him, and to the Virgin Mary, by whose intercession alone I firmly believe that I was set free. Hope, then, and the firm conviction that I had of again seeing you, sir, made me still more attentive in learning how to cure the gravel, in which I saw my master daily doing wonders; he taught me his method, and made me both prepare and administer the ingredients. Oh, how often did I wish that I had been a slave before the death of your father; for I believe that if I had known the secret I now send you, he would not have died of that complaint. I remained with this old man from September 1605 until August 1606, when he was taken and sent to try his skill on the Grand Sultan; but he died of grief on his road, and so the journey was in vain.

"He left me to one of his nephews, who was a thorough man-hater; but he soon sold me again after his uncle's death, having heard that M. de Breves, the

French ambassador in Turkey, was coming with express authority from the Grand Turk to liberate all the Christian slaves. A renegade from Nice in Savoy, a sworn enemy, bought me, and sent me to his *temat*, as they call the farm they rent under the Grand Turk; for there the people possess nothing, but all belongs to the Sultan; the *temat* of this person was in the mountains, where the country is very hot and barren. He had three wives, of whom one was a Greek Christian, but a schismatic; another was a Turk, who became the instrument of the infinite mercy of God in delivering her husband from his apostasy and restoring him to the bosom of the Church, and also in delivering me from my captivity. She was curious to know our manner of life, and came to see me every day in the fields where I was digging; and one day she ordered me to sing the praises of my God. The remembrance of the 'How can we sing in a strange land' of the captive children of Israel made me begin, with tears in my eyes, the Psalm, 'By the waters of Babylon,' and after that the 'Salve Regina,' and several other things. It was wonderful to see with what pleasure she listened; and she failed not to tell her husband that same night that he had done wrong in leaving his religion; that she esteemed it very highly, from the account which I had given her of our God, and from several hymns which I had sung in her presence; in which she said she had experienced such delight, that she did not believe the Paradise of her fathers, and that which she had hoped for, could be so glorious, or accompanied with such joy, as the satisfaction she had received while I sang the praises of my God; concluding that there must be something marvellous in it. This woman, like another Caiphas, or like Balaam's ass, made such an impression upon her husband, that he told me the next day that he should consider it a great gain if we could escape into France, and that he hoped in a few days that we should have to give God thanks for the same. These few days lasted six months, during which he sustained me with this hope; at the end of which time we escaped in a little skiff, and reached Aigues Mortes on the 28th of June; and shortly afterwards arrived at Avignon, where the Vice-legate publicly received the renegade, with tearful eyes and heartfelt sobs, into the church of St. Peter, to the glory of God and the edification of all present. This prelate has kept us both with him, intending to take us to Rome, whither he goes immediately upon the arrival here of his successor. He has promised the penitent to place him in the severe convent of the 'Fate ben Fratelli,' to which he has dedicated himself."

Such is the account Vincent himself gives of his captivity. The whole letter is characteristic of the man. Not one word of complaint, no vivid painting of the sufferings he endured; but a simple cheerful narrative, full of submission and devotion, and marked with that quiet humour which never failed him. And yet, such was his humility, that he tried his best to destroy even this simple chronicle of his early life. The circumstances under which this letter was preserved are too curious to be passed over in silence.

It was in June 1607 that he escaped from slavery; and this letter is dated from Avignon, July 24, 1607, just after the reconciliation of his renegade master. In 1658 the letter was found among some other papers by a gentleman at Dax, who gave it to his uncle, one of the canons of the cathedral in that city. The canon sent a *copy* of it to Vincent two years before the death of the Saint, thinking that the old man might like to read his youthful adventures. He read it, and he cast it into the fire; and immediately wrote to the canon, thanking him for the copy he had sent, and requesting him to send the original also. It seems that the canon did not comply with this request; for the Saint wrote again, only six months before his death, pressing him very earnestly to send the original letter. The secretary, who wrote at Vincent's dictation, suspecting that the said letter contained something which would redound to his praise, and that he only wished to get it in order to burn it as he had burned the copy, and thus to suppress the circumstance, whatever it might be, slipped in a private note of his own to the canon, begging him to send the original to some one else rather than to Vincent, if he did not wish it to be destroyed. This was done: the letter was directed to one of the priests of St. Lazarus; and thus it was preserved. He never afterwards once alluded in conversation or writing to his slavery in Tunis; although he had much to do with the care of slaves, never did his brethren nor his most intimate friends hear him mention it.

Vincent arrived at Rome, in company with the Vice-legate, towards the end of the year 1607, and remained in that city until the end of 1608. During his stay in the Eternal City, the Vice-legate made him one of his own family, and provided for all his needs. What satisfaction he felt during this time he himself recorded thirty years later, in a letter he wrote to a priest of his company then in Rome. "What consolation was it to me," he says, "to find myself in that city, the mistress of Christendom, the dwelling of the head of the Church militant, the spot where are the bodies of St. Peter and of St. Paul, and of so many other martyrs, and of holy personages, who in past times have shed their blood and spent their lives for Jesus Christ; how happy I considered myself to be in treading the very ways so many great saints had trodden! it was a consolation which affected me even to tears." Yet, with so many things to distract and divert his attention, his love for study triumphed over all, and he gladly returned at every leisure moment to the pursuits which he had engaged in at Toulouse. He did not remain long in Rome; for among others to whom his patron the Vice-legate had introduced him was the Cardinal d'Ossat, who conceived so high an opinion of him, that shortly afterwards, having a very important communication to make to the French king, which he was unwilling to commit to writing, he intrusted it to Vincent, and sent him to Paris to communicate it by word of mouth to Henry IV.

Here, again, was another opportunity of gaining distinction, which came unsought; what others had toiled to attain, Vincent found, as it were, thrust upon him. Engaged in a mission of such importance, to a king so anxious as Henry IV. to attach useful men to his person, and from one of such influence as the Cardinal d'Ossat, he needed but a short attendance at court under such circumstances to have gained high distinction. But Vincent had other views; and having discharged his mission with care and fidelity, he quietly withdrew from scenes whose splendour had no attraction in his eyes. Indeed, he seems to have taken pains to keep out of sight every thing which might tend to his advantage. For instance, he had hitherto been always called M. de Paul, which was his surname; but fearing that it might make people suppose him to be a person of good family, he had himself called for the future M. Vincent, the name he had received in baptism, and by which he was accordingly designated during the greater part of his life.

CHAPTER III.

FIRST VISIT TO PARIS.

It is interesting to meet with the descriptions which are given of Vincent at different periods of his life, it satisfies in some measure the wish so naturally felt, to see him as he appeared to his contemporaries. An intimate friend says of him at this time, when, after leaving the court, he resided for a short time in the Faubourg Saint Germain, "He seems to be very humble, charitable, and prudent; doing good to every one, and troubling none; circumspect in what he says, listening quietly to others, and never interrupting them; and ever employing himself diligently in visiting, succouring, and exhorting the poor." Such was Vincent, then, before his great work was assigned him: training himself in the school of Christ, and doing on a small scale what afterwards he was to carry out so largely; but doing it in the same spirit, with the same humility, the same quiet perseverance, the same patience, and the same cheerfulness.

During this visit to Paris a strange accident occurred, which must have sorely tried his patience, but in which he triumphed gloriously over human frailty, and proved the strength of the foundation upon which his virtue was built. It chanced that while he was lodging in the Faubourg Saint Germain, a certain country magistrate from Landes shared his chamber, and one day falsely accused Vincent of having robbed him of 400 crowns. The fact was, that the judge rose early one morning, and went out to transact some business in the city; but forgot to lock a cabinet in which he had placed his money. He left Vincent in bed; for he was unwell, and expected some medicine, for which he had sent. The apothecary's boy brought the physic, and while looking in the cabinet for a glass, saw the money. The temptation proved too great for the lad, who silently took the money and carried it away with him. When the magistrate returned, great was his astonishment to find the money gone; and upon questioning Vincent, he could get no other answer than that he had not taken it, nor had he seen any one else do so. The magistrate stormed and raged, and insisted upon his making up the loss; he drove Vincent from his lodgings, proclaimed him on all sides as a rogue and a thief, and carried his complaints to every one to whom he was known and with whom he had any intimacy; and happening to know that Vincent frequently visited Father de Bérulle, at that time the general-superior of the Oratorians, and afterwards a cardinal, he went and found him there one day in company with some distinguished persons, and in their presence accused him of this robbery. Vincent did not show any trouble or resentment at this public insult, nor did he take pains to justify himself; he merely said, in his own quiet way, "God knows the truth."

But though Vincent took no pains to vindicate himself, God did not suffer His faithful servant to remain under this imputation. Within a few years the boy who had stolen the money was arrested and imprisoned at Bourdeaux upon some other charge. He was thus brought into the province and within the jurisdiction of the very magistrate whom he had plundered. Urged by remorse of conscience, he sent for the judge, acknowledged the robbery, and promised to make restitution. The magistrate immediately wrote to Vincent to beg his pardon; he prayed him to send him his forgiveness in writing; protesting that if he did not do so, he would come to Paris with a rope about his neck and cast himself as a suppliant at his feet.

Vincent in after years turned this incident to the profit of his spiritual children; but in such a manner as to conceal his own merits, relating it as though it had befallen some other person. This was a favourite practice with him, by means of which others profited by his experience, without any prejudice to his own humility and love of self-forgetfulness. In a conference at St. Lazarus upon the subject of correction, he said: "If we have not committed the fault of which we are accused, let us bear in mind that we have been guilty of many others, and for them we ought to desire to bear this shame; and so we should receive it silently, and above all things we must avoid the expression of anger against those who accuse us.

"I knew a person, who, upon being accused by his companion of having robbed him of some money, mildly answered that he had not taken it; but seeing the other persevere in the accusation, he turned himself to God, and said to Him: 'What have I done, my God? Thou knowest the truth!' And thereupon he put himself in the Lord's hands, and resolved to give no further answer to the charge, although his accuser went so far as to take out a summons against him, and served him with a formal notice. And then it came to pass, and God permitted it, that in about six years the man who had lost the money found the thief in a distant part of the country. Behold, then, the care which Providence takes of those who trust therein. And then this man, calling to mind the injury he had done his innocent friend through his passion and evil-speaking, wrote a letter to beg his pardon; telling him that he was so angry with himself for what he had done, that he had determined to come all the way to beg forgiveness on his knees. Let us, my brethren, judge ourselves deserving of all the evil which is said against us; and let us leave to God the task of manifesting the secrets of conscience."

It was about this time that Vincent determined to live no longer among seculars, but to enter more fully upon the duties of his ecclesiastical state. Feeling unwilling to take any step in so momentous a matter merely upon his own convictions, he determined to go into retreat, and put himself under the direction of

some experienced confessor. He naturally turned to
his friends the Fathers of the Oratory, and entered
their house, where he remained about two years; not
with any intention of joining that community, but that
he might be more at leisure to learn his vocation, and
prepare for its fulfilment, under the judicious direction
of their celebrated head, Father de Bérulle. At the
end of this period the parish of Clichy, in the neighbourhood of Paris, became vacant by the resignation
of M. Bourgoing, who entered the Oratory, and afterwards became Father Superior; and, at the recommendation of Father de Bérulle, Vincent consented to
accept that parish. Two or three years previously
Henry IV. had named him, at the recommendation of
Cardinal d'Ossat, to the abbacy of St. Leonard de
Chaume, in the diocese of Rochelle; and Queen Margaret of Valois had about the same time made him
her chaplain, and in this quality had placed him over
her household. All these high offices were cast aside,
that he might devote himself to the service of those he
best loved, the poor and the little ones of Christ.

It is easy to imagine with what zeal and devotion
Vincent entered upon his duties at Clichy. Those who
knew him, tell of the incessant labours in which he
toiled for his poor flock; visiting the sick, comforting
the afflicted, relieving the poor, reconciling enemies, re-
uniting friends, recalling the negligent to their duties,
encouraging the good, becoming all things to all men,
that he might gain all to Christ. With all these many
and various duties, there was nothing like confusion or
hurry. He found time for all things; time to listen
with patience to the long and tedious narratives in
which uneducated people indulge so freely; he had a
sweet smile for those who could prize it; a gentle
manner to win the confidence of the timid; and yet
withal stern ways and severe words for those who
needed them. And while he thus laboured in rearing
up the spiritual fabric, he failed not to do what was
needed in the material church. Civil war and the

curse of religious division had for years devastated the land: souls were lost, while churches were profaned and destroyed; and he who would be a faithful pastor must gather up the scattered flock and restore the desecrated altar. Vincent did both; he who so prized the beauty of holiness, was not unmindful of what was due to the house of God. He was too jealous of his Master's honour, to leave the place of His dwelling uncared for. We soon find him entirely rebuilding the little church of Clichy; not with his own means, for he had nothing to give; nor solely by the alms of his people, for they had suffered too much in the wars to undertake so great a work. His influence remained wherever he had been; and he never wanted means to do God's work, when his needs were known.

CHAPTER IV.

VINCENT IN THE FAMILY OF DE GONDI.

In the course of about three years, namely, in 1613, Father de Bérulle persuaded Vincent to quit his parish, and to enter the family of the Count de Joigny, as tutor to his three sons. Again he submitted to the decision of his director, and left his poor and beloved flock to associate once more with the great ones of the earth. The position was important and responsible. Emmanuel de Gondi, Count de Joigny, was one of the first of the French nobility, and his wife, Frances de Silly, was as distinguished for her piety as for her high birth. Their three children were naturally marked out for high and important stations in whatever course of life they might embark; so that, in selecting Vincent de Paul for their preceptor, M. de Bérulle showed the high opinion he entertained, not only of his principles, but of his power over the minds of others. One of these children died young, the other two held a conspicuous place in history; the elder, as the Duke de Retz, succeeded to the honours of the family, and the younger, as coadjutor, and afterwards Archbishop of Paris, and Cardinal de Retz, played a prominent part in the wars of the Fronde.

Vincent spent twelve years in this family, more like a monk than a domestic chaplain, and least of all like a chaplain of those times, when civil wars, religious dissensions, and the spread of infidelity, gave a sanction to almost every excess. He made it a rule never to present himself before the Count or Countess except when sent for; and when he was not engaged with his pupils, he lived alone in his chamber; and thus, in a great house filled with people, he preserved the silence and recollection of a Cistertian. But there were other duties which drew him forth from his retirement,—calls which it was not in his nature to resist. Any good office for the spiritual advantage of another, any help in sickness or in other distress, any quarrel to be set right, any dispute to be healed (and in these fierce times, and amid the retainers of a great house, we may be sure there would be many such), would draw him from his cell, and Vincent would find enough to gratify his missionary zeal. Under his gentle influence the character of the house gradually changed,—a religious tone passed over the whole; and on the approach of great festivals, Vincent might be seen surrounded by the retainers, instructing and preparing them for Holy Communion. When the family visited any of their country residences, as Joigny, Montmirail, and Villepreux, he found fresh occupation and new pleasure in spending his times of recreation in instructing and catechising the poor, in preaching to the people, and in administering the Sacraments (especially that of penance), in which he received the cordial sanction of the bishops and the ready cooperation of the parish-priests.

Of the members of this family there was none who sympathised so fully with Vincent, or who entered so completely into all his plans for the spiritual advancement of the household or the relief of the peasantry, as the lady who presided over it. She was the first to discern his worth, and the first to put herself under his spiritual direction. Before his coming among them, she had been the protector of the orphan and the widow, the friend of the friendless, the vindicator of the oppressed. It was on the occasion of one of these visits to a country-seat, that an event occurred which ultimately led to the formation of the great institution which is the glory of Vincent's name, the Congregation of the Mission.

In 1616, he accompanied the Countess to the castle of Folleville, in the diocese of Amiens; where they remained for some time. As usual, Vincent employed himself in labours of mercy, and was one day requested to go to the village of Gannes, about six miles from the castle, to hear the confession of a peasant who was dangerously ill, and who earnestly desired this consolation. While he was on his way thither, it occurred to him that it would be safer for the dying man to make a general confession, as, although he had always lived in good repute among his neighbours, it might be a still further security for him. The result showed that this thought was a special inspiration of God, who designed to show mercy to a perishing soul, and to snatch it from the brink of a precipice; for Vincent found that he who had lived with such a fair reputation was in truth burdened with several mortal sins, which he had for years concealed through shame; and so he had lived on, making sacrilegious confessions and communions until the last, when God in His infinite mercy sent a stranger to confess him. The man made no secret of this, but openly avowed it in the presence of the Countess and of others. "Ah, madam," said he, "I should have been damned had I not made a general confession; for there were several gross sins which I had never before dared to confess."

These awful words made a profound impression upon all present, and led the Countess to exclaim, turning to Vincent: "Ah, sir! what is this that we hear? Doubtless this is the case with many other poor creatures. If this man, who had so fair a reputation, was in a state of damnation, what must be the state of those whose lives are much worse? Oh, M. Vincent, how many souls destroy themselves! and where is the remedy for this?" It was a hard question; but difficult as it was, Vincent gave it a noble answer in the institution which grew out of this day's experience, and which did for thousands what he had done for this poor peasant.

It was in January 1617 that the event occurred which has just been related; and that the good work thus begun might go on and bear fruit, the Countess requested Vincent to preach in the church at Folleville, on the Feast of the Conversion of St. Paul, upon this same subject of a general confession. The effect cannot be better told than in the modest language of the Saint himself. " I set before them," he says, " the importance and usefulness of making a general confession, and explained the best way of making it; and God regarded so favourably the confidence and firm faith of this lady—(for the great number and enormity of my sins must have checked the fruit of this good action)—that He gave His blessing to my discourse, and the good people were so moved by God, that they all came to make their general confessions. I continued to instruct and prepare them for the Sacraments, and began to hear their confessions; but the crowd was so great, that, even with the assistance of another priest who came to my aid, there was more than I could do, and so the Countess sent to beg the Jesuit Fathers at Amiens to come and help us. She wrote to the reverend rector, who came himself; but as he could not remain long, he sent another father to take his place, who assisted us in the confessional as well as in preaching and catechising; and, through the mercy of God, he had enough to do. We afterwards went to the neighbouring villages, which belonged to the Countess, and continued the same system. Every where there was a large assembly of people, and God's blessing crowned the work. Such was the first sermon of the mission, and such the success which God gave it on the day of the Conversion of St. Paul; and not without a special reason did God bring it to pass on that day."

It was Vincent's wish that this day should be celebrated by his congregation as their chief festival; each return of it was marked by him with special prayers and thanksgivings, in gratitude for what God had done by and for them, and in earnest supplication for His abiding presence. His spiritual children still celebrate this annual feast, in commemoration of this first work of their mission. But though, in one sense, it is true that the work of the mission began at this time, inasmuch as Vincent then acted upon the principle which respect; for I had fully resolved to discharge exactly all the outward duties of my profession, and to take as much care of other people's souls as I took little of my own."*

Accordingly, he took pains to conceal his licentiousness from both clergy and people, and was so decorous and guarded in his outward conduct, that the most active and learned priests of the diocese were anxious to see him promoted to be his uncle's coadjutor. To serve his political and private ends, as he himself avows, he occasionally attended, when in orders, the spiritual conferences instituted by St. Vincent; he studied theology, preached, disputed with heretics, and was liberal in almsgiving. Yet all this time, as his memoirs show, he was an artful political intriguer and an habitual debauchee. Not that he affected "godliness,"—he was too honest or too careless for that; nor that in his heart he ridiculed devotion,—on the contrary, evil-liver as he was, he seems to have entertained a real admiration for virtue and piety. But he had deliberately chosen his portion—the honours of the world, and as much of its pleasures as was compatible with the attainment of credit and power. To do him justice, he appears to have had some scruples as to degrading the priestly character in the eyes of the multitude, and thus diminishing the influence of religion and morality. This, indeed, seems to have been the one redeeming point in his character: deliberately choosing evil, he never at least deceived himself into thinking that he was other than he was, nor ceased to do homage to virtue, though he had not the will to follow it. He boasts that St. Vincent, whose pupil he had been, said of him at the beginning of his career, that though he was then devoid of all piety, he was not far from the kingdom of God. Such words from the lips of such a man are prophetic; and that towards the end of his life he sincerely repented, and became "a model of gravity, piety,

* "Memoirs of the Cardinal de Retz, written by himself" (Evans's translation), vol. i. p. 56-57.

PREFACE

disinterestedness, an...
under the grace of...
rived from the ministries...

he afterwards developed and systematised, yet full eight years intervened before the work was formally entered upon and the congregation formed. It is very doubtful whether at this time the Saint had any view beyond the present necessity; whether he did more than use the instruments which presented themselves first to his hands, to be laid aside when the immediate end was answered. But whatever may have been his ideas on the subject, it is evident that he had no intention of founding a congregation at that time; for the Countess, who acted under his spiritual direction, seeing the need of repeating this same work at regular intervals, especially among the peasantry, determined to give 16,000 livres (800*l.*) to some religious community, upon condition of its undertaking this duty on her own estates once every five years, and commissioned Vincent to carry her design into execution. In accordance with her wishes, he made the offer to Father Chartel, the Provincial of the Jesuits, who promised to write to them on the subject, and ultimately declined it. The offer was afterwards made to the Fathers of the Oratory, who also refused it. Upon this, the Countess, not knowing to whom to apply, made her will, in which she left the same sum to found the mission in whatever place and manner M. Vincent might judge most fitting. God, in His providence, had evidently reserved this particular work for our Saint, and would not permit others to take it in hand.

In July of this same year (1617), Vincent formed the resolution of leaving his friends and benefactors, and devoting himself to parochial duties. His heart all along yearned after the poor, and he seemed to feel that he was not fulfilling his vocation while he was not entirely engaged in their service. Besides, he was not content with his position in the house of Gondi. He disliked the honours and tokens of affection which he received; the high esteem in which he was held pained and distressed him; he feared lest the influence he had obtained might be but a snare to hold him back from the way of perfection. Moreover, the great assistance the Countess had received from him in her spiritual advancement, and in her many schemes for the benefit of her household and dependents, made her rely so completely upon him, that she could not rest during his absence; and thus, when any pressing necessity called him away, her anxiety was extreme lest any accident should befall him, and she should thereby be deprived of her director. Vincent feared lest she might hinder her own progress in the spiritual life by this over-dependence upon man, and felt that it might be better for all that he should withdraw; and, at every sacrifice of feeling, he quietly left Paris, and, at the suggestion of M. de Bérulle, went to Châtillon-les-Dombes in Bresse, where he entered upon his missionary labours with his usual zeal and devotion.

The distress of the family of Gondi, when they found that Vincent had left them, was great; and urgent were the letters both the Count and Countess wrote to entreat him to return. But no entreaties could move him from what he believed to be the course of duty; and it was not until M. de Bérulle and Father Bence, the Superior of the Oratory at Lyons, interfered, that he could be prevailed upon to return to a sphere of duty which he had so well filled. At last, in December of the same year, he came back, and was received by all as an angel of light. To quiet the mind of the Countess, he promised to remain as long as she lived; a promise that he faithfully performed.

Vincent's absence from Paris was but of short duration; only five months intervened between his departure from the house of Gondi and his return; and yet in that time a work was done which will be remembered with gratitude when others, which at the time made more noise, will have passed away. It was while parish-priest at Châtillon that he conceived the idea of founding the Confraternity of Charity; and, like many other great ideas, it was suggested by a very insignificant incident.

One day, when he was just entering the pulpit of the church of Châtillon to preach on a certain festival, a lady of rank stopped him, and begged that he would recommend to the charity of the congregation a certain poor family in the neighbourhood, several members of which had fallen ill, and were in extreme distress. The Saint, while complying with her request, took occasion to speak of the duty of relieving the poor, and especially those who were sick. God was pleased to move the hearts of the people, and the result was, that many of the congregation visited the poor family in the course of the day, and carried food and other gifts for their relief. Vincent himself, accompanied by a few persons, went to see the sufferers after Vespers; and not knowing that others had done the same, he was astonished to meet several parties going on the same charitable errand, others returning with empty baskets, and some resting with their loads under the trees from the summer heat. "Why," said he, "these good people are like sheep which have no shepherd. This is great charity, but not well directed; the poor people will be overloaded with provisions for a few days, and then they will be in as much distress as before." The very next day he assembled some of the most devout and affluent of the ladies of the parish for the purpose of arranging some system for the relief, not only of this one family, but of all others who might require it, and such a system as would afford them relief as long as they should stand in need of it. He spoke with his usual winning eloquence upon the duty thus set before them; and having induced them to undertake the work, he drew up for their guidance certain rules which they were to endeavour to follow, and which were afterwards to be sanctioned and confirmed by authority; and thus began the Confraternity of Charity, for the spiritual and corporal relief of the sick poor. He appointed certain officers among them, and received their report every month. This is the account Vincent has frequently given, to show by this example that the good works of his congregation have grown up, as it were, of themselves, without any forethought or design on his part, and that the work was of God and not of man.

Vincent now established two more of these confraternities; one at Villepreux, with the sanction of Cardinal de Retz, the uncle of his pupils, and at that time Bishop of Paris, and another at Joigny. The fourth was at Montmirail; and so rapidly did the desire for this institution spread, that in a very short time they were to be found in more than thirty places.

On his return to the Joigny family, he found them much in need of his help. Civil war, embittered by religious dissensions, distracted the land. Fire and sword were doing their deadly work; smoking ruins marked the sites of God's houses, while deserted and half-desolated villages showed too plainly where hostile armies had passed. What wonder, then, if the poor were uninstructed, when death had deprived them of their teachers! Famine stalked through the land, and laid its gaunt hand upon those whom war had spared; and then came the pestilence, which ever follows in its footsteps. Thus the labour of the priest increased as his strength diminished, and his assistants died around him. It was but a natural impulse which drove men into the great cities, for there alone were to be found food and protection; and the necessary consequence of this was the terrible neglect and abandonment of those who remained behind in the villages. A man whom Vincent was trying to deliver from heresy argued from this state of things against the truth of Catholicism. "Sir," said he, "you have told me that the Church of Rome is guided by the Holy Spirit, but I do not believe it; for I see, on one side, poor Catholics in the country abandoned by their pastors, and so ignorant of their duties that the greater part know not even what the Christian religion is; while, on the other hand, I find the cities and towns filled with idle priests and monks, who do nothing; and perhaps there are in Paris ten thousand such, who leave these poor country-people to perish in such disgraceful ignorance. And you wish to persuade me that the Holy Spirit directs a body of men like this—I will not believe it." There was great exaggeration in this terrible picture; controversy never understates its case; and he who looked with unfriendly eyes upon the Catholic Church, and could find no argument to justify his schism but what he built upon the faults of Catholics, would naturally run into excess when describing those faults. But allowing for all this, and deducting considerably from his account, there still remained enough to cut to the heart one so jealous of God's glory, and so tenderly attached to the poor as Vincent de Paul. He felt that there was only too much truth in the statement; and while, in reply to the Huguenot, he showed that things were not as bad as he represented them to be, and that, even if true, the conclusion he deduced from them was false, he failed not to take the matter seriously to heart, and resolved to devote himself still more completely to remedy such evils. Vincent told him he was ill-informed as to what he said; that many parishes possessed good priests and good curates; and that among the ecclesiastics and regulars, who abounded in the cities and towns, there were many who went regularly to catechise and to preach in the country, while some were continually engaged in prayer to God and in singing day and night the praises of the Lord; and others, again, were of great use to the public by the books they wrote, the doctrines they taught, and the Sacraments they administered. And even if there were some who did nothing, yet that, after all, they were but individuals liable to err, and that they did not constitute the Church. He added, that when he said that the Church was guided by the Holy Spirit, it was to be understood generally, when it was assembled in councils, and in particular when the faithful followed the light of faith and the rules of Christian justice: and as for those who turn from these things, they resist the Holy Spirit; and although they may be members of the Church, they are nevertheless of the number of those who live after the flesh, and who shall die, as St. Paul says.

This answer, though more than sufficient to meet the difficulty, failed for the time, and the man remained in his schism. But when Vincent returned next year to the same neighbourhood, with the Archdeacons of Chartres and Beauvais, and other priests and regulars, to carry on the work of the mission, the Huguenot came to the religious exercises. He saw the care taken to instruct the ignorant, and was impressed with the charity which bore so patiently with the dulness and slowness of these poor people. He watched with astonishment the effect upon their hearts and minds of what they were with such difficulty taught. Hardened sinners converted into tearful penitents, men who had lived without God crying, as in apostolic times, "What must we do to be saved?"—all told, too plainly to be misunderstood, that God was in the midst of His people, and that those who preached and taught with such fruit were working in His power and might. His heart was touched; he bowed before the Divine presence, and coming to Vincent, he said, "I see now that the Holy Spirit directs the Roman Church, which thus cares for the instruction and salvation of these poor villagers; I am ready to enter the Church whenever you are willing to receive me." Vincent thereupon asked him if he had any remaining difficulties. "No," said he; "I believe all that you have told me, and am ready to renounce publicly all my errors." After some further inquiries, to test his knowledge and acceptance of the truths of the Catholic faith, Vincent appointed the following Sunday for his reception, and directed him to attend at the church of Marchais, near Montmirail, where the mission would then be held, to receive absolution from his heresy. He attended at the time appointed; and at the close of the morning sermon Vincent, having informed the congregation of what had occurred, called the man by name, and demanded of him before them all if he still persevered in his wish to abjure his heresy, and to enter into the bosom of holy Church; to which he replied, that he persevered; but that one difficulty had arisen in his mind with respect to a rude stone image which represented the holy Virgin: "I will not believe," said he, "that there can be any power in that stone," pointing to the image opposite to him. Vincent replied, that the Church does not teach that there is any virtue in these material images, except when God pleases to communicate it to them, as He can do, and as He did to the rod of Moses, which worked such miracles; and this any of the children present could explain to him. Whereupon he called one of the best instructed, and asked him what we ought to believe respecting holy images. The child replied, "That it is good to have them, and to render them the honour which is their due, not for the sake of the material of which they are made, but because they represent to us our Lord Jesus Christ, His glorious Mother, and the other saints of paradise, who, having overcome this world, exhort us by their silent forms to follow them both in their faith and in their good works."

Vincent was satisfied with this answer, as was the Huguenot. But the Saint expressed his dissatisfaction at the difficulty thus raised, seeing that the man had been fully instructed before upon this as upon all other points of the Catholic faith; and therefore, not considering him in the due disposition to make his abjuration, he delayed it until a future day. In due time he again presented himself, renounced his heresy publicly before the parishioners, made profession of the Catholic faith, and persevered to the end of his life. Vincent years afterwards related the circumstances of this conversion to his congregation, to encourage them in the labours of the mission, concluding his narrative in these words: "Oh, what a happiness it is to us missionaries, to prove that the Holy Spirit guides the Church by working, as we do, for the instruction and sanctification of the poor!"

CHAPTER V.

VINCENT AMONG THE GALLEY-SLAVES.

A NEW field of labour now opened on Vincent, in another part of the country, and among another class of people. It has been mentioned that the Count de Joigny was general of the galleys. Feeling the responsibility of his office, he was at length most anxious that Vincent should see to the souls of those poor creatures who were committed to his charge. With this view, he solicited of the young king, Louis XIII., the office of royal chaplain to the galleys for Vincent. The king gladly made the appointment; and Vincent at once started for the scene of his new labours, that he might judge for himself of the wants of the prisoners. He reached Marseilles in 1622. A frightful sight met his eyes when he entered the prisons. Bodily suffering was bad enough in such a place, where toil seemed incessant and without alleviation; but the misery and horror of the scene were augmented tenfold by the unabashed vices of the inmates. The noise of labour was drowned in the din of blasphemy, and the foul air of the unwholesome prison was purity itself as compared with the moral pollution that prevailed. It was a terrible spot, where spiritual degradation rendered physical suffering only the more repulsive, and the punishment with which crime was visited did but brutalise what it should have reformed.

Vincent threw himself at once into his new task, and with heroic courage met and conquered what would have appalled any heart less stout and true than his own. He quailed not at the hideous sight, nor shrank from the awful blasphemies and imprecations which met his ears; for he saw in these poor sinners those only

for whom his Lord had died. And yet to impress
their hearts, to win their attention to what he had to
say, seemed almost a hopeless task, so debased and
brutalised were they by suffering and sin. With sweet
words, and gentle winning ways, he went amongst
them. He kissed their chains; he embraced them;
he listened patiently to their complaints; he used
prayers and remonstrances to induce those in charge
to deal more tenderly with them; and thus in various
ways he showed his sympathy and affection. The result answered his hopes. Those who had stood firm in
their sins, and who turned a deaf ear to the words of
rebuke, could not hold out against so novel an assault.
Hard words and rough blows they could bear un-
moved; but tears and entreaties fairly overcame them.
Beneath the cold unfeeling habit of sin was the warm
human heart; and Vincent's love could penetrate to
its innermost recesses; his gentle words found an echo
within, where such sounds had been so long unheard.
The savage men learned to weep like children; and
those who had mocked and blasphemed knelt humbly
at prayers which came from the lips of one who had
shown how tenderly he loved them.

In a short time he worked a wonderful change in
the galleys. When he came, he could compare them
only to hell, such were the sounds and sights which
filled them; when he left them, they were what prisons
should ever be, places in which contrite souls did penance, and in which a loving and gentle submission
sanctified the punishment which the law imposed.

After a time Vincent returned to Paris; but only to
carry on more completely the work he had begun at
Marseilles. He visited the places in which convicts
were confined before they were sent to the galleys, and
found them, if possible, still worse than those he had
just quitted. The system seems to have been, to cast
these unhappy creatures into the Conciergerie, or some
other prison, and to leave them for years in utter neglect, devoured by vermin, half-starved, and utterly

exhausted in mind and body, until at last they were sent to the galleys. Here accordingly Vincent found the work more within his own power. At Marseilles he was only the royal chaplain, who could but advise and suggest what in the end he must trust to others to follow up or to neglect; in Paris he could carry out what he devised. With the assistance of the general of the galleys, he at once began to ameliorate the condition of these poor outcasts; and with this view, he took and fitted up a house in the Faubourg St. Honoré, near the church of St. Roch, into which the prisoners were removed; and here they were kept until their removal from Paris.

Vincent now gave full reins to his charity; visiting the prisoners daily, instructing and preparing them for the Sacraments. Sometimes he remained for days together in the midst of them, especially on one occasion, when there was a fear of some contagion prevailing. When, at times, he was obliged to absent himself, that he might attend to other matters, he placed two of his friends in charge over them, who lived in the house with the convicts, and said Mass for them.

About this time (1623), the war which was raging made it advisable to remove the galleys from Marseilles to Bourdeaux, where they would be more secure. Hither Vincent followed them; and that the work of amelioration and reform might be carried out more effectually, he associated with himself several religious of different orders, who divided the galleys among them, and visited them in parties of two. Great fruit followed this mission; and Vincent, on his return to Paris, brought with him a Turkish convict whom he had converted, and who was baptised with the royal name of Louis, the Count de Joigny standing as godfather.

CHAPTER VI.

VINCENT AT MACON.

THE new route he had to travel brought Vincent into a fresh scene for the exercise of his zeal and charity. His road lay through Macon; and that city was about to feel the influence and power of an energy which quailed before no difficulty, and shrank from no labour of love. Macon had at this time a very bad name. It was infested with beggars of the lowest and vilest description; idle, dissolute crowds swarmed in its streets, blocked up its church-doors, and terrified alike the peaceable inhabitants and the passing traveller. Misery enough was there throughout the length and breadth of France,—real, inevitable misery, which the fierce civil war had brought upon the innocent and good; and cities like Macon, with their trade destroyed, and their intercourse with other places well nigh interrupted, must, of necessity, have suffered severely. It was as much as charity could do to meet these pressing wants, and to keep from actual starvation those who, through no fault of their own, suffered in their country's afflictions. At such a time vice and idleness became far more terrible and mischievous than usual; for they consumed what virtue pined after, and diverted from their true course the alms which were then most needed. And under this twofold affliction of silent misery and clamorous idleness did Macon labour: its virtuous poor were numerous, but its dissolute beggars were still more so; and, as is too often the case, the importunity of the latter filled the public ear, while their eager hands grasped nearly all which charity could bestow. The natural consequence of such a state of things followed: people grew weary of relieving those whose idleness was evident, and whose vice was notorious;

and so relief grew less and less, and men learnt to shut
their hearts and hands against those who had so little
claim upon their bounty. Then the noisy throng grew
fierce and riotous; and fear bestowed what justice would
have withheld. Alas for the silent grief-smitten sufferers! they had before been robbed of their share by
these evil-doers, and now the reaction which comes of
charity abused and alms perverted told with full force
upon them. Hard enough had they found it to lay
open their griefs to generous fellow-townsmen; but how
shall they now face those who have grown suspicious
and impatient?

Such was the state of Macon when Vincent de Paul
arrived there on his way to Marseilles. Under ordinary
circumstances he would have passed on; for he had
work enough before him, and why should he turn aside
or linger on his road? But there was something in the
very aspect of the place which spoke to his heart, and
told him that he had a labour of love to perform for
which time must be found. Could he traverse those
narrow streets without observing the misery which
crowded them?—or could he pass through the hideous
swarm of the idle and profane which beset the very
doors of the churches, without marking the clamorous
oaths and fierce bearing which demanded rather than
begged for alms? Here was misery enough to wring
any heart; so we need not wonder that it pierced Vincent to the quick, or that he set himself at once to the
work which stood thus ready to his hand. But one
might suppose that there would be a difficulty in his
way,—which, however, Vincent does not seem to have
felt, though it occurs naturally enough to the mind of
the reader,—and that is, what will the ecclesiastical authorities of the city say to this interference on the part
of a stranger? And it so happens that Macon had not
a few such within its walls; indeed, it abounded in
high dignitaries, as the chronicles of the time fail not
to tell us. First, there was Louis Dinet, the bishop;
then, no less than two reverend chapters; for Macon

had, like London and Dublin, its abbey-church as well as its cathedral; and the canons of the former were, moreover, of high nobility; no one who was not a noble, and a "noble of four generations," could be admitted into its august body. Now what would all these high and mighty personages—bishop, deans, chapters, and noble canons—what would they say to the passing stranger who lingered on his road to do what they had left undone, and to set their city to rights? But Vincent knew how to overcome greater obstacles than these. In truth, he had a wondrous skill in winning over to his purpose all who came in his way; and these high dignitaries were soon to add the momentum of their influence to his active exertions, and to bear them and him triumphantly to success. But when he began his work he was alone; and little encouragement did he receive as he went from door to door, pointing out the misery and degradation of the poor mendicants, and soliciting alms and other assistance from the citizens. Some people laughed in his face, and pointed at him in mockery in the streets; and even prudent people thought his scheme impracticable; the more courteous bowed him out, while the ruder sort shut their doors in his face.

Yet the Saint still persevered. Then some suspicious people began to see a political plot in the movement, and their sagacity discovered in Vincent its secret agent; and so men grew more jealous of the importunity of this meddling stranger, who would not let Macon alone. Thus difficulties seemed to increase; but the heart of Vincent felt no misgivings. He knew well what he was about; his experience was brought to bear upon a work which was no sudden effort of ill-directed philanthropy; and he knew, moreover, in Whose cause he laboured. He had his reward. By degrees men began to think there was something in what he suggested; and perhaps they felt ashamed of their own indifference in the presence of so ardent an advocate. Thus he won his first converts; a little money came into his hands, and a few citizens joined him in the work of reformation. The tide turned; popular opinion, at first so adverse, now veered round: men no longer closed their ears and hands against his appeals; all saw wisdom, where once they would see but folly: and now, to their credit be it recorded, they strove to make amends for past neglect by zealously co-operating in the movement. All came over to Vincent's side; bishop, canons, dean, provost, and clergy strove with the magistracy and laity (who were headed by the lieutenant-general) in a generous rivalry who should be foremost in ridding Macon of its ill name, and in converting and providing for its host of beggars.

Vincent was now in his element. With the sanction of the highest authorities, he drew up a scheme to relieve both the bodily and spiritual wants of these poor creatures, and to destroy the vicious system of beggary which had produced such miserable fruits. It would be difficult to believe the accounts we have received of the gross ignorance of this degraded class, did it come to us upon less trustworthy authority than that of Father Desmoulins, the Superior of the Congregation of the Oratory at Macon, who himself took an active part in the scheme which Vincent organised. It requires his assurance that he learnt the condition of these poor creatures not from report, but from his own observation, to credit the statement, that he found people upwards of sixty years of age who frankly acknowledged that they had never been to confession in their lives. "When we spoke to them," he adds, "of God, of the Most Holy Trinity, of the Nativity, Passion, and Death of Jesus Christ, and of the other mysteries, it was a language which they had never heard!" We need not stay to dwell upon the rules which Vincent gave to the society he thus founded. Suffice it to say, that the measures he took were proportioned to the magnitude of the evil: he caused a list to be drawn up of all the poor who desired to remain in the city, who were to receive alms on certain days; but if they should be found begging in the church, or at the doors of the houses, they were to be punished by being given some labour to do, and were to receive no alms. Those who were not residents were to be lodged for a night, and sent on the next day with a penny. The poor who were ashamed to beg were to be assisted in sickness, and provided with nourishment and needful remedies.

Such is the merest outline of a scheme which worked so well in Macon. It was for Vincent to devise the plan, to overcome first difficulties, to set it on foot, and then to leave it to others. He gave the first alms, and then went. Yes, Vincent had done his work. Three weeks had he spent in Macon, and had achieved in that short time what neither clergy nor laity had dreamed of doing. He had swept the city clear of its throng of idle beggars, not by a stern law, which drives into obscure corners the misery it seeks not to relieve but only hates to look upon, but by providing those who needed them with food and clothing, as well as with the eternal Food which perisheth not. He had recalled the inhabitants, both high and low, to a sense of their duties; and if it is to their disgrace that such want and ignorance should have been in a city so largely provided with clergy and magistrates, let it also be remembered to their honour that they did not hedge themselves up in their pride and reject the rebuke which a stranger's zeal must have given them; but that they frankly confessed their fault in the most effectual manner, by joining him zealously in his plans of amelioration, and by continuing the good work which he had begun amongst them.

Vincent left them; but how? Like one whose work had failed, and who fled in shame from the scene of his discomfiture! He learnt that the people had determined to send him away in triumph. They had laughed at his zeal and mocked at his scheme but three weeks before; and now they are in tears at the thought of his departure. If he must go, it shall be with all the city in his company. The high dignitaries, who had looked so coldly upon the meddling stranger, are to do honour to his farewell; and surely the citizens, who have profited by his zeal, and his beloved poor, who recognise in him a spiritual father, and who owe him more than tongue can tell, will grace his triumph, and usher on his road to Marseilles the lowly and gentle-hearted priest. All is arranged; but Vincent spoils every thing. For while they are making ready, and, doubtless, settling the knotty question of precedence among the numerous dignitaries, he quietly steals away, and is far from Macon ere the arrangements are completed. The Oratorians, with whom he stayed, alone know of his departure. He had taken an affectionate farewell of them the night before, and did not expect to see them again; but their love would not suffer him to depart without one last word of greeting: they entered his chamber in the early morning, and, while bidding him adieu, they marked, what their sudden entry had not given him time to conceal, that the mattrass was not in its place, and that he had slept upon the bare boards. In his confusion he tried to cover the mortification by some excuse; but the good fathers knew how to appreciate the deeds of saints, and bowed in loving reverence before the servant of the Lord.

CHAPTER VII.

VINCENT AND ST. JANE FRANCES DE CHANTAL.

It was in the year 1622 that Vincent accepted the office of spiritual director to the nuns of the Order of the Visitation of St. Mary at Paris. This order had been founded some years previously by the great Bishop of Geneva, St. Francis de Sales, who, about this time, sent Madame de Chantal to establish a house at Paris. Humanly speaking, the success of the work depended chiefly upon the wisdom, prudence, and discretion of the spiritual director: this no one understood better than that great discerner of spirits St. Francis; and therefore we may easily imagine what care he would take to select the right person for so important an office. There were many in Paris at this time of high reputation for learning, wisdom, and sanctity; doctors of the Sorbonne, and of the great university; parish-priests of name, and others who gave themselves wholly to the direction of souls; and yet St. Francis passed over all these, and fixed his attention upon Vincent de Paul. Knowing well the humility of the man, St. Francis overruled by anticipation his refusal of the office, by obtaining a positive command from Cardinal de Retz, the Bishop of Paris.

Our Saint, as had been foreseen, shrank in dismay from the task assigned him. Labour in the Lord's vineyard was what he sought and loved. When the poor needed him, he went with cheerful and ready heart; for his home was among them, and his great humility found its safest shelter in their lowly dwellings. Here, however, was another task, a different kind of work, and one to which he thought himself unequal. But what could he do? St. Francis de Sales asked for him; St. Jane de Chantal needed his spiritual guidance; and his ecclesiastical superior, the Cardinal de Retz, insisted upon a Saint complying with what Saints required. There is a peculiar interest in the great names thus brought together: no less than three canonised saints uniting in one particular work, and arranging together the foundation of a religious house. Seldom is it that God pours so bountifully upon one spot His choicest gifts, or brings together on earth those who in so supernatural a degree are fulfilling His will. It was, indeed, a blessing for Paris to hold such treasures within its walls, while religious and civil dissension was preying upon the life of the nation. Vincent bowed to the decision of his Bishop; and when he had once accepted the office of director to this new house, he threw himself with his usual zeal and energy into the good work. As might be expected, the new order quickly took root, and flourished under such rulers; the first house speedily gave birth to a second; and then a third grew up; and in a few years a fourth appeared; and all these in Paris, and all under the direction of Vincent de Paul. For thirty-eight years we find him continuing the same good offices, and with what fruit the history of the order plainly shows. St. Francis de Sales lived not long to carry on the work which his piety and zeal had founded; but he had the consolation of leaving it in the hands of Vincent, and well did he know the value of him to whom he had intrusted an institution so dear to his heart. It was not mere report, or the language of others, upon which the mutual knowledge and esteem these two Saints had of each other were founded. They had met in Paris, and had there formed a close intimacy; and the testimony the Bishop of Geneva gave of his friend was this: "I never knew a man more wise or more holy than he." And as with St. Francis de Sales, so was it with the venerable mother who, under his direction, presided over the order. Madame de Chantal recognised at once in Vincent one who would supply the place of

St. Francis, and be a father to her young foundation. She placed herself in his hands, and for the twenty years which she lived after his appointment she sought no other director and looked for no other guide. Even when the requirements of new houses called her away from Paris for a time, she failed not to communicate with her director by letter; and several of these touching memorials of her fervent devotion and profound humility are still preserved. The following is one of them:

"So you are engaged to work, my very dear father, in the province of Lyons; and thus we are deprived of the sight of you for a long time. But to what God does we can say nothing, but bless His name for all things, as I do, my dearest father, especially for the liberty that your charity has given me of continuing to confide in you, and of troubling you with my affairs; and this I shall do as frankly as possible. I have spent four days in the spiritual exercises; I could not give more time, because of the many matters which forced themselves upon me. I have seen the need which I have of cultivating humility and self-sacrifice for my neighbour,—virtues which I took in hand last year, and which our Lord has given me grace to practise a little; but He it is who has done all, and who will yet do this, if it shall please Him, since He gives me so many opportunities. As to my state, I believe that I am simply waiting for what it may please God to do with me; I have neither desires nor intentions; nothing influences me but the wish to leave God to act; and however little I may see my way, this is at the bottom of my soul: I have neither view nor opinion as to the future; but I do at the present hour what seems necessary to be done, without thinking of what is more distant. Oftentimes all is in rebellion in the weaker part, which causes me much distress; but then I know that 'in patience I shall possess my soul.' Moreover, I am wearied to excess in my charge; for my spirit greatly hates action, and necessity forcing me thereto, my body and mind are exhausted; on the other hand, my imagination troubles me greatly in all my exercises, for which I feel great repugnance. Our Lord thus permits me to have many external difficulties, to the end that nothing in this life may please me, except the will of God alone, to which He wishes mine to be conformed. May He have mercy upon me! I beg you to pray earnestly for me; and I will not fail to pray, as I do with all my heart, that He will strengthen you for the charge which He has given you."

We have recorded, under Vincent's own hand, the opinion which he entertained of this holy woman; wherein, among other virtues which characterised her, he especially mentions, that humility, mortification, obedience, zeal for the sanctification of her holy order and for the salvation of the souls of the poor, showed themselves in her in a supreme degree. "In a word," he adds, "I never perceived any imperfection in her; but a continual exercise of all sorts of virtues." He concludes the formal document we have just quoted by the following extraordinary relation: "I have no doubt that God will one day manifest her sanctity, as I believe has been already done in several parts of this kingdom and in different ways, of which the following is one which happened to a person worthy of trust, and who, I am sure, would rather die than tell a falsehood. This person had received intelligence that the end of this holy woman was approaching; thereupon he knelt down to pray for her, and the first thought which came into his mind was to make an act of contrition for the sins which she had committed, and which she commonly committed; and immediately afterwards there appeared to him a small globe, like fire, which rose from the earth and advanced to meet another larger and more brilliant orb; the two united, and then rose still higher to enter and combine themselves with a third infinitely larger and more luminous than the others: and it was told him interiorly that the first globe was the soul of Madame de Chantal; the second, that of St. Francis de Sales; and the third, the Divine Essence: and that the soul of the first was united to that of the second, and both to God. Again, the same person, who was a priest, said Mass for Madame de Chantal immediately after he had heard the news of her happy departure; and being at the second memento, where one prays for the dead, he thought that it would be well to pray for her, as, perhaps, she might be in purgatory on account of some words which she had spoken at a certain time, and which seemed to trench upon venial sin: at that very moment, he saw once more the same vision, the same globes, and the same union; and there remained in his mind an interior conviction that her soul was blessed, and had no need of prayers; and this has remained so imprinted on the mind of the priest, that he seems to see her in this state whenever he thinks of her. What may raise a doubt respecting this vision is, that this person has so high an opinion of the sanctity of this blessed soul, that he never reads her letters without tears, through the conviction which he has that God inspired her with what they contain; and this vision might consequently be the effect of his imagination. But what makes one think that it is a true vision is this,—that he is not subject to such things, and never had but this one. In faith of which I have signed and sealed this document."

The priest thus spoken of was Vincent himself. To him the vision was vouchsafed, and upon the *fact to* which it testified the Church has since set her seal by the canonisation of Madame de Chantal. That mind must indeed be sceptical which can doubt the reality of this vision. Vincent was not the person to be misled by his imagination; one possessing a mind so thoroughly practical as his, so well versed in the direction of religious, and therefore so alive to the presence of mental delusions and so skilled in detecting them, was not likely to be the victim of fancy; while the calm reasoning tone in which the narrative is told is in itself a pretty

sure token of the state of mind in which the vision was
beheld. We may safely conclude that God was pleased
thus to comfort the mind of His faithful servant with
a revelation of the glory into which that blessed soul
had entered which he had guided so well. Nor was
the vision in respect to St. Francis de Sales without its
especial consolation to Vincent. We have seen how
these three Saints combined in bringing to Paris the
new Order of the Visitation; and now two of them had
passed away. Vincent alone was left; natural, therefore, was it that his tender heart should yearn after
those who had thus worked with him in the vineyard
of the Lord, and that his great humility should shrink
from the responsibility which they had hitherto shared
with him. The gracious Master whom he served would
not leave him without comfort, but chose to make this
special revelation in order to show him the reward his
friends had obtained, and to remind him that they were
now his advocates in heaven, and would one day share
with him the crown which this good work had gained.

CHAPTER VIII.

THE COUNTESS DE JOIGNY AND THE NEW ORDER.

It is some time since we have spoken of the Countess de Joigny; but we must now return to her, for she has a great work in hand, in which Vincent plays a most important part. No new work, indeed, is it, nor one which comes before us for the first time; but it is the fulfilment of a long-cherished desire, and the realisation of a scheme very dear to her heart. We have seen the many efforts she made, in 1617, to induce some religious order to carry on the missions which Vincent at that time began among the peasantry upon her estates; how she had laid aside a large sum of money, not less than eight hundred pounds, to provide for the expenses of such a mission; and how she had applied to both the Jesuits and the Oratorians to undertake the task, and applied in vain, because God had destined this particular duty for Vincent de Paul. Time had passed on, and year after year the good Countess renewed the gift in her will to whomsoever God might appoint to the mission; for she seems to have had no misgivings as to its ultimate adoption, and had learnt to wait the time of her Divine Master. And now, after seven long years, she attempts again to carry her plan into effect; if not in the way she had at first intended, at least in a modified form. If no existing order would undertake the work, she thought that some provision might be made to continue it in the way it had been begun. She saw that several ecclesiastics were in the habit of assisting Vincent in the missions he gave; and she hoped that if a house were set apart in Paris for the use of those who thus worked with him, some of them might permanently live there, and receive from time to time others who were willing to devote themselves to the same duty. By these means the good work would be perpetuated, and her design carried out. Before taking any steps in the matter, she consulted her husband; and he not only approved of her plan, but insisted upon becoming a joint founder with her; and to complete the work, they went together to the count's brother, the Archbishop of Paris. John Francis de Gondi had lately succeeded his elder brother, the Cardinal de Retz, in the government of the diocese of Paris, which had under his rule been raised into an archbishopric. Like the rest of his illustrious house, he was well acquainted with the virtue and zeal of his sister-in-law; and when she laid her scheme before him, he not only gave it his cordial approbation, but undertook to provide the institution with a fitting habitation; and gave at once the College des Bons Enfans for this purpose. The next thing to be done to carry into effect the noble design, was to appoint a superior equal to the work; and of whom but Vincent could they think? Here was their only difficulty; for they knew that his humility was as great as his other virtues, and they foresaw how he would shrink from taking this responsible office upon him. So they determined that they should all three—archbishop, count, and countess—see him, and cut short all the excuses which he might urge. This they did, and the lowly servant of God bowed before the authority of those who ruled as much by affection as by power; the priest obeyed his ecclesiastical superior, the chaplain his earthly patrons, and the man yielded to the wishes of those whom he had long learned to love for their charity, and to venerate for their self-denial. He consented to the three things which they required of him: first, that he should become superior of the college, and take upon him the direction of the priests who might live there with him, as well as the general superintendence of the missions; next, that he should, in the name of these priests, accept the money which was to endow the house; and thirdly, that he should appoint those whom he might think fitted and disposed for such a work. The affair being thus arranged, no time was lost in carrying it into effect; and in a few days, on the 1st of March 1624, the Archbishop drew up the patent for the headship of the College des Bons Enfans. On the 17th of April the Count and Countess de Joigny made over the money for the endowment of the new institution, in a deed which we must quote at some length, because it so well illustrates the high principles which actuated them, and the end they proposed to themselves.

The document begins by declaring, first, "that God having inspired them for some years past with the desire of doing Him honour, as well on their own estates as elsewhere, they have considered that, since it has pleased His Divine Majesty to provide in His infinite mercy for the spiritual necessities of cities, by the number of holy doctors and virtuous religious who preach and catechise therein, and who preserve in them a spirit of devotion, there remain only the poor country-people to be cared for. They think that this can be remedied by a pious association of certain ecclesiastics of known orthodoxy, piety, and fitness, who are willing to renounce preferment in cities, as well as all appointments and dignities in the Church, to apply themselves, under the superintendence of the Bishops, simply and entirely to the salvation of these poor people; to pass from village to village at the expense of their common purse, to preach, instruct, exhort, and catechise the poor, and to bring them to a general confession, without taking from them any payment or offering whatever, to the end that they may distribute without charge the gifts they have gratuitously received from the hand of God. To make provision for this end, the said count and countess, in thanksgiving for the benefits and graces which they have received, and still daily receive, from the same Divine Majesty, to assist in the salvation of poor souls, which God so ardently desires, to honour the mysteries of the Incarnation, Life, and Death of our Lord Jesus Christ, out of love for His Most Holy Mother, and, moreover, to strive to obtain grace to live

well the rest of their days, that they may come with
their family to eternal glory,—to this end the said
count and countess have given as alms the sum of forty
thousand livres (2000*l*.), which they have delivered in
cash into the hands of M. Vincent de Paul, priest of
the diocese of Acqs, for the following purposes: that is
to say, the said count and countess have given and do
give to the said Sieur de Paul the power of electing
and choosing within a year such a number of ecclesiastics as the revenue of the present endowment can
support, whose orthodoxy, piety, good morals, and in-
tegrity of life are known to him, to labour in the said
work under his direction as long as he may live; and
this is the express will and intention of the said count
and countess, both on account of the confidence which
they have in his management, and from the experience
they have had of the good effected in the said missions,
in which God gave him an especial blessing. But notwithstanding this direction, the said count and countess
intend that the said Sieur de Paul shall make his continual and actual residence in their house, that he may
continue to them and to their family the spiritual assistance which he has rendered them for so many years.

"The said ecclesiastics, and others who desire or
who shall hereafter desire, to give themselves to this
good work, shall devote themselves entirely to the care
of the said poor country-people; and to this end they
shall bind themselves neither to preach nor administer
any sacrament in cities which are the seats of bishops,
archbishops, or of courts of justice, except in cases of
extreme necessity. The said ecclesiastics shall live in
community, under obedience to the said Sieur de Paul,
and to their future superiors after his death, under the
name of the Company or Congregation of Priests of the
Mission. Those who shall be hereafter admitted to this
work shall be bound to the intention of serving God in
the aforesaid manner, and of observing the rule which
shall be made upon this point. They shall be obliged
to go every five years through all the estates of said the

count and countess, to preach, to hear confessions, to
catechise, to do all the good works aforesaid, and to
assist spiritually poor prisoners, that they may turn to
profit their bodily pains. Thus shall the said count, as
general of the galleys, satisfy the obligation by which
he feels himself bound; and this charity he intends to
be perpetuated towards the convicts by the said ecclesiastics, for good and just considerations. Lastly, the
said count and countess shall remain joint founders of
this work, and, with their heirs and successors of the
same family, shall for ever enjoy the rights and privileges which are conceded and granted to patrons by the
holy canons; except the right of nomination, which they
have renounced."

There are some other clauses in this deed, which relate to the rules to be observed by the ecclesiastics
during the missions, as well as at other times, which are
too long to be given here. Enough, however, has been
quoted to explain the object of the institution, and the
spirit which actuated its pious and noble founders.
There is one point which must not be overlooked, and
which shows in a wonderful way the complete disinterestedness of these truly great people. There is not one
word from beginning to end which binds the new order
to say Masses, either for their patrons or for their
family. They claim no share in the good works; they
require no prayers for themselves; they leave the missionaries free, that they may apply themselves un-
shackled to the work assigned them, and that all may
be absorbed in the one important duty. Thus was the
anxious wish of the good countess fulfilled, and the great
work begun which God had especially designed for Vincent. Small in its beginnings, and limited in its first
action to a minute portion of France—indeed, almost to
the estates of a single nobleman, it rapidly developed,
and quickly spread itself beyond the limits of the land
which gave it birth. And now, in two centuries, it has
passed into all lands, and the children of St. Vincent are
to be met doing their Master's work wherever God

calls them and their burning love for souls can find a sphere.

The Countess de Joigny died shortly afterwards. It seemed, indeed, as though the labours and trials of her life were to end with this good deed, and she was at once to enter upon her reward. Scarcely had two months elapsed after the signing of the deed of foundation, when she was seized with her last illness; and on the Feast of St. John the Baptist the soul of this noble lady passed to its eternal rest. Vincent was there to assist her with the many consolations and aids which holy Church provides so bountifully against that last time of trial; but her husband was away in Provence, busied with the duties of his high station. She died in peace, as those must die who live, as she lived, in the fear and love of God. In her high station she had been ever mindful of the duties and responsibilities which belong to a wider and more influential sphere. The mother had trained her children by her own bright example, and by providing for them such a tutor as Vincent de Paul; the wife had inspired her noble husband with a generous rivalry in works of mercy; the mistress had won the affections of her retainers, and turned that influence to their eternal gain; while the ruler over wide domains had sought out the poor and needy, whom others cared not for, and had provided as well for their eternal as for their temporal wants. In hard stern times, when the worst passions of human nature were let loose, and many a man's hand was raised against his brother,—when the rage of civil war and the violence of heresy set at variance those whom God had joined in closest ties,—when the land was blackened with ravage and profaned with sacrilege,— the pure charity and untiring zeal of the Countess de Joigny came like a fair vision over the scene. Her presence put to flight sin and blasphemy; she brought succour to the distressed, consolation to the afflicted, and that priceless sympathy which cheers the heart and strengthens it against severest trials

History would indeed be intolerable, were not its darkest pages brightened by such lights as these; lights which remind us that all is not evil, and that God's ministers are silently working even where Satan holds such mighty sway. What heart but would faint at the terrible tale of war and rapine, of deceit and cruelty, which blots so many pages of each nation's annals, were it not conscious that amidst it all there are those who quietly undo much of the evil which the sinful passions of men inflict upon the world, and who in some measure alleviate the miseries which apparently prevail without mitigation or relief? To such a glorious work was the good countess called; and how well she fulfilled it we have to some extent been able to see. More might have been told, but such was not her wish: she was content to leave her many noble deeds concealed with God; and He who leaves not the cup of cold water unrecompensed which is given in His name and for His sake, will in the great day remember and reward the good works of the Countess de Joigny.

CHAPTER IX.

THE COLLEGE DES BONS ENFANS.

VINCENT was now about to enter upon the great work of his life; that work which is more especially connected with his name, and for which, one might say, he had been so long in training—for Vincent was no longer a young man. There is something very significant in the fact, that eight-and-forty years of his life had been spent before his chief work was begun. We might have thought that fresher powers and younger energies were needed for so great an undertaking; but God judges not as man; and He who entered not upon His public ministry until the last few years of His human life, giving thirty years to preparation and less than four to teaching, was pleased to lead Vincent in His own divine steps, and to keep back the great mission of the Saint until his later days. Not that the life he was just entering upon required any abrupt change; it might rather be regarded as the completion and perfection of what had gone before. Step by step had he been led on, circumstance after circumstance had conducted to the one end; and he who had laid down no plans for the future, who had aimed at nothing but to do God's will as it came before him, found himself, at the end of nearly fifty years, in a position to do a great work for God's glory, and with powers fitted for the task intrusted to him. Let us pause a moment, to cast a hasty glance over the life which we have thus far traced, and see how all things worked together, not only for good to one who so loved God, but in an especial manner to fit him for the work on which he was about to enter.

The poor peasant boy, who fed sheep amidst the dreary *Landes,* never forgot the class from which he sprang; their spiritual wants were his life-long care; he was ever mindful of his lowly birth, and failed not at proper times to recall it to himself and others. When, in later years, he was raised to so high a position under the queen regent that every great ecclesiastical appointment passed through his hands, and the high and noble paid court to the humble priest, he failed not to remind them that he was but the son of a peasant, who had once fed swine. The poor student, obliged to teach others that he might have wherewithal to pursue his own studies, was unconsciously in training for the preceptorship of the young scions of the house of Gondi, whereby he entered into the first labours of his great mission, and formed so enduring a friendship with the founders of his future society; while the prolonged course which he was enabled to go through at the University of Toulouse prepared him for the spiritual direction of his community and the effective working of his spiritual retreats for the clergy. Did his career seem interrupted and his studies frustrated by his captivity and slavery in Barbary? Yet this it was that made him so well acquainted with the condition of slaves, and enabled him so successfully to carry out his designs of charity in their regard. His deliverance from captivity led him to Rome, and placed him under the eye of Cardinal d'Ossat, who sent him to Paris on a special embassy to the king, and thus brought him into personal contact with Father de Bérulle and the family of Gondi. If he left that house for a time, it was that he might found his Confraternity of Charity; and when he returned, it was to originate the great order which bears his name. Through all, as well in what has been mentioned as in other circumstances which have not been specified here, we may trace the hand of God, "sweetly disposing all things" to the great end for which Vincent was designed; while he, the humble and self-distrusting servant of God, looking neither to the right hand nor to the left, but doing zealously and to the best of his power whatever came in his way, fulfilled his part in the task of preparation; and so, when at length the work was ready to his hands, he was found worthy to receive it. Abelly, St. Vincent's best biographer and his intimate friend, who resigned the bishopric of Rodez that he might join the Saint in the new mission, has drawn us a portrait in full length of Vincent at this time, which we will partly give:

"In person he was of middle height and well formed; his head was somewhat large, but well proportioned to the rest of his body; his forehead broad and commanding, his face neither too full nor too thin; his aspect was gentle, his glance piercing, his hearing quick, his deportment grave, and his gravity benign; his countenance was simple and unaffected, his manners very affable, and his disposition extremely kind and amiable. His temperament was ardent, and his constitution strong and robust; nevertheless he felt severely changes of seasons, and was very subject to fevers. His mind was large, well balanced, and circumspect; capable of great things, and difficult to be taken unawares. He never entered lightly into any investigation; but when he had once seriously taken a matter in hand, he laid it bare to the very bone; he weighed every circumstance, whether great or small, he anticipated the inconveniences and consequences which would arise; and yet, for fear of deceiving himself, he did not decide at once unless he was pressed to do so; and he came to no conclusion until he had carefully weighed both sides, and was even then very glad to consult others. When he was obliged to give advice, or to come to any decision, he laid open the question with so much order and clearness, that he astonished the most expert, especially in spiritual and ecclesiastical matters.

"He never was in a hurry; no matter how numerous or how complicated were the affairs which he had in hand, nothing put him out; but with indefatigable zeal he entered upon them, and with equal perseverance he went through the work. When he had to discuss any question, he listened willingly to others; never interrupted any one while speaking, and yet patiently submitted to interruptions, stopping short at once, and again resuming the thread of his discourse. When he gave advice on any matter, he never spun out what he had to say, but expressed his thoughts in clear and concise language; for he had a natural eloquence, which enabled him not only to explain himself briefly and with effect, but also to touch his hearers, and to persuade them by winning words when he was endeavouring to do them good. In every thing he said simplicity was combined with prudence: he spoke plainly of things as he judged them, and yet he well knew how to be silent when it would be unsuitable to speak; he was always guarded in his remarks, and was careful never to say or write any thing harsh or irritating, or which might be taken to express any bitterness or disregard of others, or to argue want of respect or of charity towards any one whatever.

"His disposition was very averse to changes, novelties, and singularities; it was a maxim of his, that when matters are well one ought not easily to unsettle them under pretence of making them better. He distrusted all new and extraordinary propositions, whether speculative or practical, and held firmly to common uses and opinions, especially in religious questions; on this subject he said, 'The human mind is active and restless, and the cleverest and most brilliant are then only the best when they are most cautious, while those advance with certainty who never wander from the way in which the multitude of wise men have gone.' His heart was most tender, noble, and generous, easily won by all that was good and holy; and yet he had a most perfect control over all its inclinations, and subjected his passions so perfectly to reason, that scarcely could they be perceived to exist."

It is not necessary to follow Abelly through all the details of the picture he has painted so minutely, and with all the affectionate anxiety of an attached friend; nor need we dwell long upon the elaborate defence which he makes of Vincent against the two faults which some attributed to him: namely, that he was over-slow in determining matters and in carrying them into execution, and that he spoke too ill of himself and too well of others. For these are just the complaints we should expect to hear from those who could not imitate his quiet ways, and who are too ready to sit in judgment upon all and every one. Vincent de Paul needs no apologist. That he should be misunderstood by people who mistook haste and confusion for industry and diligence, was but natural; such minds cannot separate labour from noise, and many duties from much distraction; quietness with such is but another name for idleness, patience but intolerable slowness, consideration but procrastination; and yet, had they but considered the amount of work Vincent did in his quiet way, the time he saved which they wasted in fretting and fuming, they would have learnt to think differently of him in this respect, and would have admired his skill in doing so much with so little show, and in so quietly fulfilling the many duties which fell to his share.

As to the other complaint, that he spoke too ill of himself and too well of others, it must be confessed that herein Vincent set himself in opposition to the general practice of the world, which has a very different rule of action. To put forward all they can in praise of themselves, and to conceal all that tells against them, is a rule which is limited to no one class or age of men. It may show itself more undisguisedly in children and among the ruder sort; but it lurks no less surely under habits the most refined. The covert allusion to self, and the skill which glides so rapidly over what is not to our praise, illustrate this rule as truly as the loud boasting of the vulgar and the falsehood which conceals our shame. Vincent's practice was just the contrary to this; and herein it was that he gave offence to many. Had he been content to go half-way, to have said simply nothing about himself, they might have been satisfied; but they could not endure that he

should speak ill of himself, and so frequently call to
mind his own faults. Perhaps for an ordinary Christian this would be the safer and therefore the wiser
rule; but saints are not to be judged like other men,
for this, among other reasons, that temptations which
overcome the less perfect have no power over them.
Thus there is danger of vanity under the form of humility in self-condemnation, when he who uses it has not
advanced far in self-control. He who willingly and
ostentatiously calls himself a sinner is not always ready
to endure the name when others give it to him; nor
can he at all times bear with equanimity that those
who hear his humiliating words about himself should
quietly accept them as applicable and true. There is
too often pride at the bottom, and that none the less
real because it is "the pride which apes humility."
But with men like Vincent there is no such danger.
They who have learned to look into their own hearts,—
who have courage to gaze stedfastly upon what reveals
itself therein,—who know really what sin is, and what
God thinks of it,—will never speak lightly of its burden. From such as these the acknowledgment of their
sins is wrung by a sense of justice and a love of truth.
They know what they are in their own eyes and in
their Maker's; and they shrink in horror from words
of praise, and hasten to confess what they really are,
lest they should seem to accept the terms which others
apply to them. But it may be said, How can these be
saints, if they are sinners? is it not a contradiction in
terms? No one is without sin save God Incarnate and
His Blessed Mother; but the more God's servants are
free from sin, the more terrible does sin become in their
eyes; faults which to others scarcely seem worthy of
observation are to them of great moment; and slight
imperfections, as the world judges, come out into view
in the strong light of a purified conscience, as the motes
which fill the air at all times are made visible by the
bright rays of the sun. Hence the language which saints
use when speaking of themselves is not exaggeration, or

the wish to appear worse than they believe themselves to be; but it is the knowledge of what they really are, as contrasted with what God would have them to be, which forces them to cry out, "God be merciful to me a sinner." Our judgment of ourselves depends upon the standard we make our test: he who aims low will think well of himself; but he who makes God's law his rule will have a different reckoning. The saints judge themselves as God will judge them; they anticipate in all its unerring strictness the last judgment, and they are confounded at their own unworthiness.

Pride can find no hiding-place in a heart thus scrutinised; its influence cannot tinge the colours which paint the sins of the really contrite. But where pride dwells, the language of humility is mere affectation; and he who in such circumstances calls himself the worst of sinners, in his heart denies the truth which his tongue utters. Vincent, in his freedom from pride, could with safety speak thus of himself; while to ordinary Christians the safer rule may be simply to keep silence, and to say nothing in self-praise or self-condemnation. The less self is forced upon others, the better for all. If our example will profit, it will effect its purpose in silence; if we have done well, our reward will not be increased by our proclaiming our good deeds; if we have done ill, God knows, and will judge us.

As to the other part of the charge against Vincent, that he spoke too well of others, little need be said. It follows necessarily from the former; for he who is severest in judging himself is ever gentlest in dealing with others. Of course, his own explanation was a different one: "There are some people," he said, "who always think well of their neighbour, as far as true charity will allow them, and who cannot see virtue without praising it, nor the virtuous without loving them." Such was his own case; but so prudently did he act, that he scarcely ever praised any of his companions to their face; but he never hesitated to encourage others, by rejoicing in the graces they had received, and by congratulating them upon God's goodness in their behalf. He would deal to others the mercy which God had dealt to him. He knew how easily words and actions are misunderstood, and hence he was cautious in judging, and very slow in condemning. When there was room for a good motive, he gave credit for its influence; when he could not speak favourably, he simply kept silence. Of course, when rebuke was needed, he did not withhold it, for his was a true and not a spurious charity; but as soon as possible he turned from it to do what was so much more congenial to his tender and loving heart, to speak kindly to all, and to rejoice with them in the goodness and mercy of the Lord.

But it is time that we turn from this consideration of Vincent's character to the actions which helped to mould it, and which in a measure took their colour from it. The great tie which bound Vincent to the house of Gondi was now removed. The countess had gone to her eternal crown, and the promise which the Saint had given had been fulfilled; for he had been with her to the last. Immediately upon her death, he hastened to convey the mournful intelligence to the Count de Joigny; and well did he fulfil the task, for which he was so especially fitted alike by nature and by grace, of comforting and supporting the bereaved husband in the first hours of his distress. As soon as possible he obtained that nobleman's permission to give himself entirely to the work which the liberality of this family had endowed, and in 1625, he took up his residence in the College des Bons Enfans.

Very humble and modest were the beginnings of what in time was to become so great and renowned. There was one whom God had given to Vincent years before, and who had worked side by side with him in all his missionary labours ever since; one whom he loved with all the earnestness of his tender heart, and who had been to him in its highest and holiest sense a brother. This was M. Portail, who joyfully followed the Saint to the new field of labour. These two holy men invited a third to join them, to whom they gave a stipend of fifty crowns a-year; and the three might be seen setting forth from their new residence to carry on the work of the mission. They had no servant to leave in charge of the college, and so Vincent locked the door and left the key with some neighbour until their return. Thus they went forth, carrying the few things they needed for their rustic altar and for their own support, and passed from village to village, catechising, preaching, hearing confessions, and fulfilling the various functions of the mission in simplicity, humility, and charity. They asked for nothing in return, and even refused what was offered; being mindful of the pious intention of their founders, that they should literally fulfil the divine command, " Freely ye have received, freely give." The first scene of their labours was the spot where the mission was founded, and afterwards they extended their care to other parts of the diocese of Paris.

Such was the mustard-seed from which the lofty tree of the Congregation of the Mission sprang. Well might Vincent marvel at the rapid growth of the work, and say, as he did one day to his community at St. Lazarus: "We went forth in singleness of heart, and without any thought beyond obeying the Bishops who sent us, to preach the gospel to the poor, as our Lord had done. This is what we did; and God on His part did what He had foreseen from all eternity. He blessed our work; and when other good ecclesiastics perceived this, they begged permission to join us; not that they came all at once, but from time to time. O my Saviour, who could ever have thought that such results could have sprung from the condition in which we once were! If any one had then told me what would be, I should have thought that he mocked me; and yet it was in that way that God willed our company to begin. Can you, then, call that human which no man had ever thought of? For neither did I nor did poor M. Portail ever dream of such a result; alas, we were very far from having any such thought!"

Shortly afterwards two other priests joined them, whom we find associated with Vincent and M. Portail in the deed of foundation, which was signed on the 4th of September 1626. In the following May, Louis XIII. issued letters-patent confirming the foundation, and permitting "the said association and congregation of Priests of the Mission to live in community, and to establish itself in such places in France as may seem good, and to accept all legacies, alms, and offerings which may be given them." It was not long before the number of this infant community was increased to seven, and thereby Vincent was enabled to carry on more extensively the work committed to his care; and that he might have courage to persevere under all the difficulties which beset a new enterprise, God's Vicar on earth blessed the work, and gave it his formal sanction. In 1632, Urban VIII. issued a bull by which he erected the company into a congregation, under the title of Priests of the Congregation of the Mission, and placed it under the direction of Vincent, to whom his Holiness gave power to draw up and consolidate rules for the right ordering of this congregation. Afterwards, to set the civil seal on what had already received the highest ecclesiastical sanction, the king issued fresh letters-patent, in May 1642, which were verified by the parliament in the autumn of the same year.

And now Vincent's first care was to train his brethren for the due performance of their especial work. He foresaw the dangers of the mission; and his task was to strengthen them, that they might stand firm under temptation. Like a wise builder, he would dig his foundations deep; and knowing that the spiritual edifice could not rest secure unless it was built upon the most perfect humility, he took every opportunity of extolling and enforcing that virtue. A trivial circumstance served to call forth one of his most impressive exhortations on this subject. One day, a priest, who had just joined the congregation, in speaking of their body, called it "this holy congregation." Vincent stopped him at once, and said: "Sir, when we speak of the company, we should never make use of this term 'holy,' or of any equivalent one; but we should rather say, This poor company, this little company, or such-like. In so doing we shall imitate the Son of God, who called the company of His apostles and disciples a little flock. Oh, that God would give this poor company the grace to establish itself firmly in humility, to dig deep and build upon this virtue, and to keep itself stedfastly therein! My brethren, let us not deceive ourselves; if we have not humility, we have nothing. I speak not only of outward humility, but more especially of humility of heart, and of that which leads us truly to believe that there is no one on earth more unworthy than you and I, and that the company of the Mission is the most contemptible of all companies, and the poorest in regard both to the number and the condition of its members, and that it well merits to be thus regarded by the world. Alas! do you wish to be highly esteemed? What is this but to desire to be unlike the Son of God? This is intolerable pride. When the Son of God was on the earth, what did men say of Him? and how did He wish to be accounted of the people? As a fool, as a seditious person, as a sinner, as less than man, though He was far otherwise. In like manner, He willed to be set aside for Barabbas, the robber and murderer. O my Saviour, how will Thy humility confound sinners like myself at the judgment-day! Let us beware of this, we who go on missions and preach to the world. Oftentimes one sees the people deeply moved by what is said, sometimes even to tears; and it may chance that they cry out, as of old, 'Blessed is the womb that bare thee, and the paps that gave thee suck!' as I have heard them do. When we hear this, the natural man is satisfied, and vanity springs up and flourishes if we do not repress this vain delight, and seek purely the glory of God, for which alone we ought to labour;—

yes, purely and simply for the glory of God and the salvation of souls. If we have any other end but this, we preach ourselves, and not Jesus Christ. When a person preaches to gain applause, to be praised, to be esteemed, or to be spoken of, what does he do?—this preacher, I say, what is his act? A sacrilege; yes, a sacrilege! What! make the word of God and things divine a mere instrument of ambition, a means by which to gain renown! 'Tis sacrilege. O my God, give grace to this poor little company, that no one of its members may ever fall into such a sin! Believe me, gentlemen, we shall never be fit to do the work of God, unless we have a profound humility, and an utter contempt of ourselves. No, if the Congregation of the Mission is not humble, if it is not convinced that it can do nothing of moment, and that it is rather fitted to ruin all than to succeed in any thing, it will never do a great work; but when it shall live in the spirit I have described, then, gentlemen, it will be ready for the purposes of God; for it is such instruments as these that God uses to work His great and real blessings. Several commentators, in explaining the gospel for this day, which speaks of the five wise and the five foolish virgins, apply the parable to those who live in community and have given up the world. If, then, it is true that half these virgins, that is, half the community, are lost, alas, how greatly ought we to fear, and I especially! Let us take courage, gentlemen, and let us not lose heart; let us give ourselves to God with a good grace, let us renounce ourselves and our own inclinations, our ease and our vanities; let us consider that we have no greater enemy than ourselves; let us do all the good we can, and do it as perfectly as we can. It is not enough that we assist our neighbour, that we fast, pray, and work at the missions; we do well herein, but there is something more to be done; we must do all in the spirit of our Lord, in the way in which our Lord did the same, humbly and singly, that the name of His Father might be glorified and His will done

"Trees will not produce better fruit than the stock from whence they spring; and we are in some sense the stock of those who come after us, who in all probability will not go beyond us. If we have done well, they also will do well, and the example will pass from one to another; those who remain will show those who come after the way of virtue in which their predecessors walked, and these will teach it to their successors; and this they will do by the aid of the grace of God, which the first members merited for them. Whence comes it that we see in the world certain families which live so well in the fear of God? I have one especially in my mind, among others, of which I knew the grandfather and father, who were both very prosperous; and to this day I know that the children are the same. And whence comes this? Simply because their fathers merited for them this grace from God of a good and holy life, according to the promise of God Himself, that He will bless such families to the thousandth generation. But, on the other hand, you may see husbands and wives who are in good circumstances and live well, and who yet ruin and destroy every thing in their hands, and succeed in nothing. And whence comes this? It is the punishment which their forefathers merited from God for their grievous faults passing upon their posterity, according to that which is written, that God will visit the sins of the fathers upon the children to the fourth generation. And although this applies principally to temporal goods, yet still we may take it in some sense with respect to things spiritual; so that if we observe our rules with exactness, if we exercise ourselves thoroughly in all the virtues befitting a true missionary, we shall in some measure merit this grace of God for our children, that is, for those who come after us, that they may do well, as we did; and if we do ill, there is much reason to fear that they will do the same, and still worse; for nature ever lags behind, and tends always to decay. We may look upon ourselves as the fathers of those who come after us: the company is as yet in its cradle, it is but just born, it has existed but a few years; is it not, then, in its cradle? Those who come after us in two or three centuries will look upon us as their fathers; for those who are in the first century are as the first fathers. When you wish to lay stress upon any passage in the writings of any Father of the first ages, you say, 'This passage is mentioned by such a Father, who lived in the first or second century;' in the same manner they will say, 'In the time of the first priests of the Congregation of the Mission they did this,' or 'they lived thus;' or again, 'such and such virtues were flourishing.' Such being the case, gentlemen, what an example ought we to leave to our successors, since the good which they will do depends in some measure upon what we now practise! If it is true, as some Fathers of the Church say, that God compels fathers and mothers who are lost to witness the evil their children do on earth, that their torment may be thereby increased; and the more these children advance in wickedness, the more these parents, who by their ill example caused those sins, suffer the vengeance of God; while, on the other hand, St. Augustine says that God causes good parents to see in heaven the good their children work on earth, to the end that their joy may be made greater:—in like manner, gentlemen, what consolation and joy shall we experience, when it shall please God to let us see our company doing well, abounding in good works, observing faithfully the appointed order of time and occupation, and living in the practice of those virtues which our good example has set before them! Wretched man that I am! who say and do not. Pray to God for me, gentlemen; pray to God for me, my brethren, that God may convert me. Let us give ourselves wholly to God, let us work in earnest, let us go and assist the poor country-folk, who are waiting for us. By the grace of God there are among us priests who are always working, some more and others less, at one mission or at another, in this village or in that. I remember once, when returning from a mission, as I drew near to Paris it seemed as though the gates of the city ought to fall upon and crush me; and seldom did I return from the mission without this thought coming into my mind. The reason of this was, that I seemed to hear within me some one saying, 'You are going back, while there are other villages expecting the same assistance which you have just rendered to this one or to that; if you had not gone thither, it is probable that such and such persons would have died in the state in which you found them, and have been lost and damned. If you have found such and such sins in this parish, do you not think that similar abominations are committed in the neighbouring one, where the poor people expect a mission? And you are going back, you are leaving them; if they die in the meanwhile, and die in their sins, you will be in some measure the cause of their ruin, and you ought to fear lest God should punish you.' Such were the distractions of my mind."

It was by such teaching as this that Vincent fitted and disciplined his fellow-labourers for the arduous task God had intrusted to their zeal. For five years did this small community continue its labour of love in the humble way we have described, doing its work quietly and unostentatiously, making little show in their poor dwelling, and attracting but little notice in the great city. Yet were there eyes scanning closely their works of charity, and tongues ready in fitting season to tell of what these servants of God were effecting. In truth, they were doing their Master's work, looking only to Him for help and comfort, thinking little or nothing of the great world around them, and therefore they won that Divine Master's care; they served Him who is never served in vain, they put themselves in His hands, and soon we shall see how He cared for them.

CHAPTER X.

THE PRIORY OF ST. LAZARUS.

THERE was at this time in Paris a house of the Canons Regular of St. Augustine, bearing the name of St. Lazarus. Its revenues were large, and its buildings in accordance with its dignity and means. There seemed little in common between the poor college of Les Bons Enfans with its obscure community, and this stately convent with its dignified ecclesiastics; indeed, they scarcely knew of each other's existence, and slight chance there appeared of any thing bringing them together. If the humble missionaries passed by the priory's lofty walls, they did not raise their eyes to mark the dignity and extent of the place; while, if accident led the canons near Vincent's house, there was nothing to attract the observation of those who moved, so to speak, in a higher sphere. Yet God brought them together for their mutual gain. The manner in which this happened is very remarkable, and must be related somewhat at length. The details have been very carefully recorded by one who was an important instrument in the work, and of whose narrative we shall make use in what we have now to describe.

It appears that, in the year 1630, the Prior of St. Lazarus, M. Adrien Le Bon, had some dispute with his community. We are not told what was the subject of controversy, but merely that he had some "difficulty" with them. But from what afterwards appears, it would seem that they could not quite agree upon their manner of life. St. Augustine's rule was, of course, plain enough; but still there might be questions of detail which each community would have to determine for itself: matters small in themselves are often great in their effects; and little differences in a religious house may create such disorder in the whole system, that nothing can go aright until these are removed. In the present case the prior despaired of success, and wished to get away from what he fancied he could not remedy. There was no great difficulty in effecting an exchange of preferment, when so high and dignified a position as that of Prior of St. Lazarus was in question. Abbeys and rich benefices were pressed upon him; and he might easily have gained, in a worldly sense, by resigning his troublesome post for one more lucrative and easy. But the prior had misgivings; after all, he might be wrong in running away from a difficult position; perhaps it was a cross which God sent him; and he knew that he who puts his hand to the plough and then looks back is not worthy of the kingdom of heaven. So he listened to the advice of his friends, and agreed to have a conference with his canons in the presence of four divines. They met at the house of one of the four; and after each side had stated its case, the prior making his complaints, and the sub-prior replying in the name of the canons, it was determined that a rule of life should be prepared which all should follow for the future. This was done; but yet the prior was not satisfied; whether the new rule was not duly observed, or did not effectually meet the difficulty, we do not know; but for some reason—and his subsequent conduct shows that it must have been a good and holy one—the prior ceased not to desire to quit his office. But, like a true-hearted man as he was, he thought more of his community than of himself; and the first question that presented itself was this, What can I do for them? How can I best profit their souls? In his anxiety he thought of Vincent de Paul and his little community. Not that he had any personal acquaintance with them; for he did not even know where they lived; but he had heard speak of certain good priests, and of the great work they had taken in hand; and he thought that if he could establish them in his priory he should have a share in their good deeds. As soon as this resolution was

formed, he hastened to carry it into effect; and calling
in his friend and neighbour Dr. Lestocq, the parish-
priest of St. Laurence, who himself relates the story, the
two set forth together to make the generous offer to
Vincent. Dr. Lestocq was a friend of our Saint's; and
doubtless it was from him that the prior learned of the
good works of the young order; and great must have
been his pleasure in bringing two such men together,
and in being thereby the medium of so advantageous
a proposal for his poor friend. On arriving at the
"Bons Enfans," the prior explained the purpose of
his visit to Vincent; telling him how he had heard of
his order, and of the great good it had wrought among
the poor; and concluded by saying that it was his
anxious wish to contribute to their holy work, and to
that end he begged to resign to their use his Priory of
St. Lazarus.

Vincent's astonishment may be easily imagined at
this unexpected offer. A rich priory, with its large
possessions and extensive buildings, suddenly cast at
his feet by one who was an utter stranger to him!
The Saint trembled; and upon the prior remarking it,
he replied, "It is true, sir, your proposal frightens me;
it is so far beyond us, that I dare not think of it. We
are poor priests, who live in a simple way, with no
other object before us but the service of poor country-
people. We are greatly obliged to you, sir, for your
good-will, and thank you very humbly for it." In
short, he showed very plainly that he had no intention
of accepting the gift, and the excellent prior was obliged for the time to content himself with this answer;
but so impressed was he with all he saw and heard of
Vincent, that he determined to renew his offer on a
future occasion, and told the Saint that he would give
him six months to consider about it. True to his word,
he returned at the end of that time, and again pressed
Vincent to accept his priory; assuring him that God
had put the idea into his mind, and that he would not
rest in peace until he had gained his end. But nothing

could move Vincent from his first resolution: he pleaded the small number of his community, which could scarcely be said to have come as yet into existence; besides, he did not wish to be talked about, and the acceptance of this large and important residence would make a great stir; and he disliked notoriety; and, in a word, that he did not deserve this favour. While he was thus excusing himself from accepting an offer which scarcely any one else would have refused, the bell for dinner rang. The prior requested permission to dine with the community; and he, with Dr. Lestocq, entered the modest refectory. Here, again, was a scene which made a deep impression on his mind, and rendered him only more solicitous for the presence of such a body of men in his own house. The simple fare; the deep silence, in which the voice of one only was heard reading aloud from some religious book, that the time given to the support of the body might not be without its food for the soul; the composed and calm demeanour of the community, quiet without the appearance of undue restraint; their countenances so mild, and yet so full of life, so devout, and yet so free from affectation; such an utter absence of sour puritanism, and yet such grave decorum,—all this went home to the heart of the good prior, who doubtless failed not to contrast it with other scenes with which necessity had made him more familiar; and natural was it that he should long for the realisation of his hope, when such order as this would be found in a more stately refectory, and others should be edified as he had been by so religious a scene.

But for some time longer it was to be the lot of M. Le Bon to sigh in vain for such a consummation, and to offer his rich gift to one who resolutely rejected it. What a picture is this! A high dignitary striving to transfer his honours to another, and that other day after day refusing them! We wonder how long the unusual contest will last, where both seem so resolute and so persevering. For a whole year the prior failed in moving Vincent; and at the last his patience seemed almost gone. "What a man you are!" he exclaimed one day, after urging once more his request; "if you will not listen to me, tell me at least to whom you will listen: whose advice will you take?" At last Vincent consented to name one to whom the friendly dispute should be referred; and he, as the prior anticipated, advised the acceptance of the offer. Great was the joy of M. Le Bon at this his final success, and no less was that of the friend who had brought the two good men together. "I could have carried M. Vincent on my shoulders to St. Lazarus!" he exclaims in a transport of joy.

On the 8th of January 1632, the day after the offer was accepted, Vincent went to take possession of his new house, and saw it for the first time. Yes, during the whole of the year in which the prior had pressed it upon him with so much earnestness, he had never once been near it! It was a large and a rich establishment, and that was enough to set him against it. Little cared he for its position, its architectural features, or its other attractions; and so, when under a sense of duty he went to live in it, no curiosity or excitement showed itself in his manner; he went quietly at once to take up his abode therein, just as he was wont to come home from a mission to his humble college. Thus was the young congregation transferred to the scene of its future labours, and the Priory of St. Lazarus received within its stately walls the humble missionaries who, as Lazarist Fathers, were to spread its name throughout the world by identifying it with their own.

It was a great place, this Priory of St. Lazarus, in more respects than one. It was great in extent, containing within its walls a magnificent chapel, and the usual buildings of a religious house on a grand scale; its domain enclosed a space of upwards of two miles in circumference, and reached to the very walls of Paris; and, moreover, it had great temporal power, for it claimed and exercised the highest and widest jurisdiction over its dependencies. In old feudal language, it was a "lordship with low, middle, and high judicature;" that is to say, its lord could hold his court, and execute judgment in all causes, from the lowest to the highest. In those times such power was something very real and tangible; and its possessor enjoyed rights and privileges which we can now scarcely understand. It is difficult to connect the simple and modest priests of the mission with the idea which all this feudal grandeur conveys. Their humble course of life, their plain rule, their loving intercourse with the poor, among whom their days are spent—all that especially characterises them seems to have nothing in common with the position in which we now find them placed. What need of a splendid church for those who are so seldom at home, and who almost daily offer the great sacrifice on the rude altar they carry with them from place to place? What use can there be in lofty halls and long cloisters for a few wearied men who return at night exhausted from the toilsome missionary tour? Vincent de Paul and his little band seem quite out of place; and one is almost tempted at first to suppose that our Saint had made a mistake in yielding to the persuasions of the prior.

So may they themselves have thought when first they left their poor college and took up their abode with the canons of St. Augustine. Yet had they confidence in their leader, whose prudence, they knew, fully matched his zeal; and so they were content to leave the matter with him who had hitherto so well directed them. Had any such misgivings crossed their minds, they would doubtless have been strengthened by a difficulty which immediately met them. The good prior was anxious, naturally enough, that his canons should profit as much as possible by the presence of the new comers; and he thought that the best way to effect this end would be for the two bodies to unite together, and to live in common. He doubtless remembered the edification which he had himself received when dining at the Bons Enfans, and he well knew the gradual but abiding effect which a good example works, and how it tells in the long run infinitely more than the best advice. So he suggested to Vincent that the two communities should in a great measure become one. And here was the Saint's first practical difficulty. It was not that he doubted for a moment what must be done; but he felt a delicacy in refusing the prior's request. His small community had been received with open arms by those who so unmistakably expressed their love and reverence for them; and here, as his very first act, he had to refuse what seemed so reasonable a request. It was a sore trial for his gentle loving nature to mark with a discourtesy his advent among them, while his humility must have suffered by an act which looked somewhat like spiritual pride. Yet, when the interests of his order were at stake, Vincent knew no hesitation: personal feelings, the wish to oblige, and the fear of misconstruction, must all be set aside when his own good sense pointed out a plain course of duty; and so he plainly told the prior that it could not be as he wished. He explained to him the rule by which his order was guided: he showed how severely it would press upon those who had not been called to such a life, and how unreasonable it would therefore be to expect the canons of the house to receive it; while at the same time he pointed out how impossible it would be for two bodies of men to live in complete community who follow a different rule, how those who observed the stricter practice would suffer by the presence of the others, while the latter would fail to derive advantage from association on such terms.

And, indeed, the rule of the missionaries was a severe one to flesh and blood. One point alone will suffice to illustrate this. Let us see what it enjoined in respect to the observance of silence. Not a word was to be spoken while they remained in the house from the hour of night-prayer until dinner-time of the following day. After dinner one hour's conversation was allowed; then silence was to be again observed until after supper, when another hour was given to relaxation; and then once more the rule had force. Thus, with the exception of these two hours, a solemn silence was observed in their house continually; no word was spoken save when necessity required, and even then what was said was uttered in the fewest words, and the lowest tone. So important did Vincent consider this portion of their rule, such stress did he lay upon its observance, that he was prepared to sacrifice all the advantages his order might derive from their new home rather than abandon or relax it: " I would rather," said he in one of his letters on this subject, " that we should live on in our poverty than that we should run counter to God's design regarding us." He well knew the danger which attends out-door employment, the distractions which the world presents to those who move in it even to do God's work; and therefore he would train his society at home in silence and recollection, that they might be prepared to overcome such temptations when they went forth to their special labours. "True missionaries," he was wont to say, " ought to be Cistertians at home and Apostles abroad." The good prior submitted to the decision which thus excluded his canons from some of the benefits which he anticipated for them, and welcomed with graceful courtesy and loving heart the founder and his order, who thus entered like conquerors on their own terms; and all seemed settled.

But now another difficulty presented itself in an unexpected quarter. Royal sanction had already set its seal upon the work, and the parliament was about to record the patent Louis XIII. had granted, when a certain religious community put in a claim to the estate. This claim, however, was soon set aside; and indeed it would not have called for notice, had it not served to illustrate the charity and disinterestedness of our Saint. Where was Vincent while the question was being decided which was so seriously to affect the well-being of his young order? He was no recluse, no dreaming visionary, but a very plain matter-of-fact personage, as the reader must long since have observed; and so we might naturally enough look for him among the lawyers and councillors, furnishing them with evidence, and helping forward his case with all his wonted skill and energy. But we should seek him there in vain: if we would find him in this important hour, we must leave the court of law, and enter another portion of the royal palace; and in the Sainte Chapelle, so rich in holy memories and in monuments of God's grace, we shall find him absorbed in prayer and in divine contemplation. Yes, he had learnt a holy indifference, and there awaited calmly the result. One thought alone seemed to trouble him, and this but more strongly marks his complete unselfishness. When he came to St. Lazarus, he found there three or four poor idiots, whom their relations had intrusted to the care of the prior. Vincent's first request was that he might take charge of them, his love yearning for an exercise which could meet with no return on earth; and now, if he feels an anxiety about the trial, it is on account of these poor helpless idiots. He could patiently submit without a sign of regret to quit the noble mansion which he had just entered; it gave him no trouble to abandon plans which he had formed for his community; but it went to his heart to contemplate the prospect of separating from these afflicted beings, to whose service he had so joyfully devoted himself. However, he was spared this trial; the opposition was soon overcome, and Vincent remained in quiet possession of the Priory of St. Lazarus.

CHAPTER XI.

INSTITUTIONS FOR THE CLERGY.

AND now our Saint is in his new house: disputes have ceased, opposition has passed away, and the old work is to go on,—but not precisely as before; for its new home is not without its influence (as what home is?); new opportunities present themselves in new circumstances, fresh duties grow up, and require, if not a new spirit, at least a new development of the old. So was it with Vincent and his little band; their sphere of action was suddenly enlarged; they had hitherto gone on their way scarcely marked of men, dwelling in the comparative obscurity of their little convent; but now they find themselves the possessors of a noble priory, with all the powers and duties which a large domain at that time implied. Their spirit is the same, but it has to fit and adapt itself to a different order of things; it must expand with its increased resources and its wider range. And herein does its divine origin manifest itself, hereby is the spirit of the order vindicated. Were it a mere thing of earth, devised by man and dependent upon him, thrust by him into the Church, and sustained therein solely by human means, it would soon sicken and die; or at best it would remain as at its formation, incapable of development, for it would have no real vigorous life in it. Like a tender exotic, it might for a time be preserved, with watchful care and jealous precaution it might linger on a while; but once remove it from the scene of its sickly life, once let the fresh air of heaven visit it freely, and it shrinks up and withers. Not so the institution which springs up in a genial soil, which is inspired with the spirit of the Church to which it belongs, which is part and parcel of that Church, lives in its life, and is in truth one with it. Such an institution requires no external nurture, depends on no foreign support, and needs no special indulgence to foster its growth. Planted in the Church, and nourished by the divine life which the Church imparts, it is ever at home; within the narrowest limits it can do its work, and when its sphere is enlarged it expands with that sphere. Wonderful is its power of self-adaptation; no stern, unbending rule eats out its life, no fetters manacle its strong limbs, no unloving eye watches its every movement to trammel and restrain its vigour. And why is this freedom? Because it can be trusted, because it is known, and because it is loved. It is doing its proper work, and so it can be trusted; it is but the continuance of what, in one form or another, has been from the first, and therefore it is known; its fruits abide and are rich in blessings to all who care to gather them, and therefore it is loved.

Such are the religious orders in the Church. Each one has its own peculiar work, yet all combine in the one great purpose for which the Church exists; each opens an especial field in which men may do that to which God has called them, while all are indeed one in unity of purpose. Thus every portion of the Lord's vineyard is duly cultivated; for each finds labourers such as it requires, and He who sends them guides and blesses them in their immediate work. Need we stay to show how such a system of division of labour ensures the completion of every part, or to point out how healthful and vigorous is the action which results from so wise a dispensation? In such a system every thing grows up naturally and in due order; nothing is forced or out of place; no abortive attempts are made, because the right people undertake the right work; and no one rushes out of his own place to strive vainly to supply wants to which others are better fitted to minister. And thus it is, that while men are labouring in what God has given them to do, they find their work growing to their hands; what was but little when they entered upon it, as time goes on expands and widens into a mighty enterprise, which, had they seen the result when they began, they might not have dared to undertake; but while it has grown their powers have grown too, and at last they find that they have been made equal to the work for which they were, unknown to themselves, from the first designed.

Thus was it with Vincent de Paul: he had gone on from day to day with no other purpose than to do God's work heartily and diligently; troubling himself but little with thoughts or plans for the future, he was content to busy himself with that which he had immediately in hand, whatever it might be; and thus his missionary efforts grew from small beginnings into the great order which bears his name.

If, as we said, his companions might have had misgivings when they first entered the stately priory of St. Lazarus lest they were going beyond their means in occupying so lofty a sphere, it was not long before they had occasion to observe how well their new residence could further the great work they had in hand, and enable them to extend its influence over a wider field. It was true that they had room enough and to spare in its spacious courts; but quickly were those to come who were to find in them a temporary home in an hour when they most needed it. Shortly before his arrival at St. Lazarus, Vincent instituted the religious exercises for the candidates for holy orders; but it was not until the larger resources of this new residence gave him the means of receiving the young ecclesiastics into his house, that that system could be completely carried out. The suggestion of these exercises is due to the pious Augustin Potier, Bishop of Beauvais, one of Vincent's best and truest friends. The heart of this zealous prelate had long been grieved at the unsatisfactory state of his clergy. He felt the necessity of increasing the number of those who were to minister at the altar, while at the same time he dreaded sending the unworthy to fill so momentous an office. Where was he to find those on whom he could lay such

PREFACE.

t; for I had fully resolved to an..
itward duties of my profession
care of other people's souls as (

:cordingly, he took pains to con..
rom both clergy and people, an
uarded in his outward conduc...
nd learned priests of the dioce..
m promoted to be his uncle's ...
olitical and private ends, as ...
ionally attended, when in ord..
:es instituted by St. Vincent; ..
hed, disputed with heretics, .
giving. Yet all this time, as .
an artful political intriguer
hee. Not that he affected "
ionest or too careless for that :
diculed devotion,—on the cor."
he seems to have entertained ..
ie and piety. But he had de..
ion—the honours of the world.
sures as was compatible with th
it and power. To do him just..
) had some scruples as to degrad..
acter in the eyes of the multitud..
ing the influence of religion and ..
ied, seems to have been the one ..
iis character: deliberately choosi..
east deceived himself into think..
er than he was, nor ceased to do ..
ugh he had not the will to follow
t St. Vincent, whose pupil he had b..
he beginning of his career, that tho..
oid of all piety, he was not far from
1. Such words from the lips of
phetic; and that towards the end .
ily repented, and became "a model ..

* "Memoirs of the Cardinal de Retz, w.
ans's translation), vol. i. p. 56-57.

minister to it; a want had to be supplied, and who
more ready and willing for the work than he whose
capacity for love was equalled only by his energy in
fulfilling love's offices? Amid the distractions and cares
of active life, man needs continually to be reminded of
his chief concern: self-examination will daily help in
this work, and meditation will raise the mind above
the world and its ends. But beyond this, it has ever
been felt needful to set apart especial seasons when this
duty is to be performed more fully and in greater detail;
and to assist those who are thus employed many spiritual
works have been written. It is also the practice of
the Church to give public sermons and instructions for
several days in succession, that those whose occupations
lie in the world may, for a time at least, withdraw
their minds from worldly cares, and devote them to the
concerns of the soul. But Vincent felt that there was
a want which these provisions did not reach; and
to meet it he now threw open his house. There are
times when each man stands more especially in need of
spiritual direction and retirement, seasons which are
the crises of his future life. No public instructions,
interrupted by worldly callings, can suffice; nothing but
the entire and absolute exclusion of the world for a time
will work the required end. What consolation to a
weary heart to find such aid and guidance at such a
time; what encouragement to the doubtful, what
strength to the weak! To such the gates of the
Priory of St. Lazarus were ever open. No question
was asked as to the rank or means of the applicant;
enough that he sought admission and wished to go into
retreat: the hospitality of the house supplied his temporal
wants, the spiritual skill of Vincent and his
brethren ministered to his soul. What a curious scene
did the common refectory present! what a strange
mixture of classes! For all who were in retreat shared
alike in the simple repast—nobles, mechanics, beggars,
ecclesiastics of high rank, and poor wandering friars,
the wise and the ignorant, the rich and the poor, each

responsibilities, and how could he test their fitness for the sacred trust? In such unsettled and disordered times, there seemed but little chance of correcting and bringing back to a sense of their duty those who had fallen into evil ways; his hopes lay rather with the young, who were just entering upon the sacred course; if he could test the vocation of these, and fit them by preparatory discipline for their sacred calling, he knew that his great object would be best attained; and so he consulted Vincent de Paul, as was his wont whenever matters of importance pressed upon him. The result of this consultation was, that Vincent went to Beauvais before the next ordination, and, assisted by some other priests, as soon as the examinations for ordination were completed gave the candidates a spiritual retreat of some days' duration; in the course of which he prepared them to make a general confession, and thus brought them in due dispositions of mind to receive the sacred orders to which they were called.

Not long afterwards the Bishop came to Paris, and so impressed the Archbishop of that city with the relation of what had been done at Beauvais, that it was determined that Vincent should receive into a ten days' retreat every candidate for ordination in Paris. And this practice has ever since prevailed in that city; while it has gradually extended to other dioceses of France, and far beyond the limits of that country. Soon were the wide walls of St. Lazarus receiving fresh inmates, who, in obedience to the Archbishop's commands, were preparing themselves by these spiritual exercises for holy orders; and thus already was a new labour of love growing up under the zealous hands of Vincent and his community. But this did not suffice him; rather did he regard these young ecclesiastics as the first-fruits of that greater band which was day by day to send its members under his hospitable roof for shelter against the storms of life, and for consolation under the weight of its trials.

There was a need felt, and Vincent was there to

minister to it; a want had to be supplied, and who more ready and willing for the work than he whose capacity for love was equalled only by his energy in fulfilling love's offices? Amid the distractions and cares of active life, man needs continually to be reminded of his chief concern: self-examination will daily help in this work, and meditation will raise the mind above the world and its ends. But beyond this, it has ever been felt needful to set apart especial seasons when this duty is to be performed more fully and in greater detail; and to assist those who are thus employed many spiritual works have been written. It is also the practice of the Church to give public sermons and instructions for several days in succession, that those whose occupations are in the world may, for a time at least, withdraw their minds from worldly cares, and devote them to the concerns of the soul. But Vincent felt that there was yet a want which these provisions did not reach; and to meet it he now threw open his house. There are times when each man stands more especially in need of spiritual direction and retirement, seasons which are the crises of his future life. No public instructions, interrupted by worldly callings, can suffice; nothing but an entire and absolute exclusion of the world for a time will work the required end. What consolation to a weary heart to find such aid and guidance at such a time; what encouragement to the doubtful, what strength to the weak! To such the gates of the Priory of St. Lazarus were ever open. No question was asked as to the rank or means of the applicant; enough that he sought admission and wished to go into retreat: the hospitality of the house supplied his temporal wants, the spiritual skill of Vincent and his brethren ministered to his soul. What a curious scene did the common refectory present! what a strange mixture of classes! For all who were in retreat shared alike in the simple repast—nobles, mechanics, beggars, ecclesiastics of high rank, and poor wandering friars; the wise and the ignorant, the rich and the poor, each order seemed to have its representative there; for the same spiritual need brought them all to those who knew so well how to minister to all. Well might Vincent say, in his own quiet humorous way, that St. Lazarus was a veritable Noah's ark, into which all kinds of animals, both great and small, were received. It was a heavy charge upon the means of the community, but Vincent knew too well its spiritual value to let any such consideration check the good work; indeed, there is scarcely any thing which he enforced more strictly upon his order than the continuance of this practice: he called it a gift from heaven, and as such he prized it.

Another want was thus supplied, another class, or it might rather be said a mighty gathering of all classes, was thus provided for; and yet the zeal of the young community was not satisfied: while any remained who could claim their aid, they seemed to feel that their work was as yet imperfect. The young ecclesiastic found a home within their walls wherein his vocation might be tried, and his spiritual armour essayed; while every man, from the highest to the lowest, secular, religious, and laic alike, might pass through the spiritual discipline of the retreat, and even those who could not have their wants ministered to within the priory were cared for in fitting place, as we shall see hereafter when we come to speak of the Sisters of Charity; for Vincent provided that the house of those holy women should be open to females, as his own priory received every man who sought admission therein. Thus the work advanced, and, like a goodly tree, it threw out its branches over all who sought its shelter, while its roots struck far and deep into the soil in which it grew.

One good work led to another; one want supplied but served to bring to light a second, which arose out of the former. The taste for spiritual food once formed, a craving grew which could not be withstood. Thus was it with those who at St. Lazarus had been prepared by spiritual exercises for the sacred ministry. They had tasted of the sweet things which holy Church provides so boun-

CH. XI.] INSTITUTIONS FOR THE CLERGY. 83

tifully for those who give themselves wholly to her service; they had been strengthened by her counsels for the warfare to which they were called; and when they went forth to the active duties of their state they naturally distrusted their own powers, and yearned after that support and encouragement which they had received within the hallowed walls. Vincent and his brethren had guided them in their preparation for the priesthood; why should they not help them still, now that they were in the midst of its engagements? They had grown to love St. Lazarus and its quiet holy ways; why should they not, from time to time, return to its calm retreat and recruit their strength? They had derived assistance from mutual intercourse; what should hinder them from meeting again, that each might bring his experience to help the rest, and that all might again go forth, with renewed energy, to bear his part in the conflict with the world and its evil ways? Such were the arguments with which they pressed our Saint; and he, of all men, was the last to throw obstacles in the way of spiritual advancement: so it was arranged that they should assemble once a week at St. Lazarus, under Vincent's direction, and hold what are called " spiritual conferences," in which they were to confer upon matters connected with their state of life, upon the ecclesiastical virtues, and upon their especial duties. The good which resulted from these conferences soon bore testimony to the wisdom which designed and guided them; and their speedy adoption in other places extended far and wide a blessing which, like so many others, flowed from the hallowed precincts of the Priory of St. Lazarus.

There is one circumstance connected with these conferences which must not be passed over, since it bears the highest testimony to the good which resulted from them, and comes from a quarter which is least open to suspicion. No one will accuse Cardinal Richelieu of too much credulity, or charge him with want of discernment in judging of those with whom he had to deal. Of course the existence of these conferences soon became known to one whose eagle glance nothing escaped; and it may be that he looked with suspicion upon regular meetings which, in days of such dark and frequent conspiracies, might have an object in view far different from the ostensible one. So he sent for Vincent, and questioned him as to his conferences. The interview was important to both and to their common country, for it brought into close union two of the most powerful men of the day, and combined them in a work which perhaps did more for the Church of France than any of the more celebrated actions which distinguished the career of the great cardinal. The modest and retiring priest stands in the presence of the renowned statesman, and to the searching questions which Richelieu knows so well how to put, he replies with a plain statement of what he had done, and for what purpose these conferences were held. If ever man could read the human heart, and pierce its innermost recesses with a glance, it was Richelieu; and now his look is turned upon that broad expansive brow, and reads in those loving innocent eyes a tale of devotion and self-sacrifice which Vincent's lips would be the last to tell. He listens with increasing interest to the account the Saint gives of his community; for the cardinal will know all, and ere the relation is concluded he has determined to use Vincent as his instrument for a great good. If the now aged statesman cannot devote time and attention enough to the selection of the persons best fitted for the high ecclesiastical offices which he has to fill, here is one before him on whom he can rely, one who has already not only brought together in these conferences the zealous young men who are just entering upon their career of duty, but has won to the same holy exercises the good and devout among the clergy of Paris. Richelieu had great faults, but none could justly accuse him of neglect or indifference in matters of this kind; it was not now for the first time that he felt the responsibility of making good appointments to important positions in the Church; and so he gladly availed himself of the disinterested advice of Vincent. He questions him as to whom he considers most worthy of the mitre; and while Vincent mentions certain names, the sagacious and prudent minister takes pen in hand, and draws up the list that he may submit it to the king. What a scene is this! The mighty statesman, who swayed France with more than royal power, whose word was law, and whose very presence awed all beholders—the great Richelieu, sits with pen in hand, and writes at the dictation of the humble Vincent the names of those whom the sovereign is to call to highest station! When did intrigue gain for its ablest master power equal to that which is here yielded to the majesty of truth and holiness? Truly do the saints possess the earth, and the humble and meek are exalted!

There was an inconvenience attending this sudden accession of power which it required all Vincent's prudence to overcome. One great object which he aimed at in the spiritual conferences was to inspire in these zealous priests a love for poverty and for the lowest stations in the Church; and now he has to select from this same body those who are to be elevated to high dignities. The line he followed was a plain and simple one, and yet full of the truest wisdom. He continued as before to inculcate the duty of self-abasement, and to inspire the spirit of humility and indifference for worldly honours; and never once so much as dropped a hint of the influence he possessed with the cardinal, nor led any one to suppose that the appointments to high office passed through his hands. So little cared he for the reputation of power; so sensitively did he shrink from all that might draw the eyes of the world upon him.

Nor was this the only good work in which Vincent co-operated with Cardinal Richelieu. The regard which that great minister entertained for him gave Vincent ready access to his presence, and, come when he might, he found him ready to listen to his suggestions, and to assist alike with his purse and influence the plans of charity and piety which Vincent had ever in hand.

We do not intend to consider in chronological order the great institutions which our Saint founded; they followed so rapidly upon one another, that little would be gained by thus arranging them. Rather would we group together those which naturally combine by similarity of purpose: by so doing we shall better appreciate each particular work when we see it in its relation to kindred objects, while at the same time we shall be able more fully to understand the completeness of the whole which these several works unite in forming. It is for this reason that we are now bringing together the several institutions which grew up in immediate connection with the house of St. Lazarus, and especially those which more directly related to the spiritual advancement of the clergy; reserving for future chapters the consideration of those corporal works of mercy, embracing alike the city of Paris and the most distant parts of the empire, which in times of deepest distress met gigantic wants with corresponding succours, and while they ministered to transitory requirements, took root as permanent institutions which time has but strengthened and extended.

Vincent has not yet done with the clergy. He has another scheme to bring before the cardinal, and, as before, he finds in him a ready and zealous co-operator. Already he has provided a retreat for those who are just about to be ordained, as well as spiritual conferences for those who are on the mission; and now there seems only one more institution needed, and that is, one in which the recently ordained, or those who are nearly ready for ordination, may pass one or two years in pious exercises, in the divine service, in studying the higher branches of theology, the ritual of the Church, the administration of the sacraments, catechising, and preaching. The cardinal not only approves of the idea, but at once gives Vincent a thousand crowns to carry it out in his old college of the Bons Enfans, and the first ecclesiastics are received there in February of the year 1642. Before long others entered the college at their own expense; and thus the *Seminary* of the Bons Enfans had its origin. Shortly afterwards similar institutions sprung up elsewhere, and Vincent saw with no small satisfaction the good work spreading and bringing forth fruit. As years passed on, this seminary outgrew the college in which it had been placed, and then Vincent removed the younger students to a house adjoining St. Lazarus, to which he gave the name of the Seminary of St. Charles, and here his own priests instructed them; a work which was long afterwards continued, and which trained up many pious youths who subsequently entered the ecclesiastical state.

This last institution completed the whole work; and thus, from first to last, from childhood till death, Vincent had provided the clergy of his diocese with spiritual nurture. The boy who entered the Seminary of St. Charles might in due time pass to that of the Bons Enfans to complete his clerical studies; the Priory of St. Lazarus received him at the end of his course for his solemn retreat before ordination; and when he had entered upon the duties of his state, the same doors were open weekly to admit him to the spiritual conferences, which strengthened and encouraged him in his arduous duties; while once a year he was called again into a longer retreat, that he might take account of his spiritual state and prepare for the end. This was the result of Vincent's labours for his brother-priests; and who shall reckon the good which Paris gained by this one work? Who shall tell what blessings the exertions of this humble priest brought upon his age and nation? When men were warring without, Vincent was toiling within; while heresy and disorder were pulling down the strongholds of religion, in the midst of tumult and blasphemy the zealous priest was quietly building up the inner temple in the souls of the faithful. Silently, and little marked of man, the holy work went

on; and when calmer moments came, and the din of
civil war had ceased, men marvelled to find what had
grown up in the midst of them, and how that obscure
man had perfected a work which should stand when
dynasties had been swept away, and should carry on
his name to times when those who in his day were
great should be forgotten or despised.

CHAPTER XII.

MADAME LE GRAS.

WE have seen what Vincent did for the spiritual requirements of his day; how he met one of its most pressing wants with institutions which insured, as far as human sagacity could insure, a due supply of learned and pious ecclesiastics. Let us now proceed to consider what he did for the temporal necessities of the poor. The reader may remember what was related in a former chapter of an institution which sprung up under Vincent's direction at Châtillon; how the ill-regulated relief of a family, whose distress he had mentioned in the pulpit, suggested to his mind the necessity of a well-organised system of succour for the suffering poor; and how he at once carried the idea into effect and founded his first Confraternity of Charity. We saw how he introduced the same system into other places; and now we have to follow up this germ of charity into its full and perfect development.

The spread of these confraternities was most rapid; and so highly did Vincent esteem them, that he made a point of instituting them wherever he gave a mission. In time they were isolated from one another, without much machinery to guide them, and left of necessity to the energy of one or two persons in each place. All that our Saint could do was to urge some of the simple villagers to undertake in some measure the care of those who stood most in need of their assistance; he furnished them with a few plain rules, and, as occasion offered, visited and helped them. But as their number increased, the time required for their superintendence was more than Vincent could spare from his other duties; and, moreover, experience showed that a female hand was needed to train those who had little but charity to qualify them for the task. It was at the very time that this want began to make itself felt, that God raised up an instrument for His purpose, and placed it in Vincent's hands for the work he had before him.

There is a name which ranks high in the annals of charity,—a name most dear to France, and one which cannot be uttered without emotion wherever the daughters of charity are known. It is that of Madame Le Gras. Placed by birth and marriage in a high position, the widow of the secretary of Mary of Medicis, she laid aside the ease and dignity of her station, and in failing health devoted her life to the service of the poor. By the advice of her spiritual guide, the Bishop de Belley, she put herself under the direction of Vincent, and took up her abode in the neighbourhood of the College of Bons Enfans in 1625, just at the time the Saint came to reside there, upon the death of the Countess de Joigny. For four years did she devote herself to works of mercy among the poor in that neighbourhood; but it does not appear that she extended her cares beyond this district. She was, as it were, in training for the greater and more extensive work that was before her, and Vincent passed her through this novitiate that her powers might be tried, her vocation proved, and the purposes for which she was designed clearly manifested: so jealous was Vincent of the instruments he employed, so cautious in testing those whom he would use, so careful lest impulse or enthusiasm should lead any to offer themselves for a work to which they were not called of God. At the end of this time, in 1629, he allowed her to enter upon the undertaking; and then it was that with well-disciplined mind and instructed zeal she made her first visit to the several confraternities which Vincent and his colleagues had founded in different parts of the country. How fraught with blessings must these visits have been to those zealous women, who in their humble way were carrying on the great and holy work! Her very presence among them must have cheered many a drooping heart, which had almost learnt to despond amid the trials and disappointments of those hard and cruel times; while the advice which her experience made so precious derived additional value from the worth and sweetness of her who gave it. Nor did she come empty-handed: money for those who were in need, clothing for the destitute, and medicines for the sick—these were the gifts which marked her presence, and which enabled those she visited to carry on more effectually the work they had taken in hand. Where confraternities were dying out, she revived and renewed them; where the labour which fell to their lot was more than they could perform, she increased their numbers; where aught was ill-regulated, she corrected and amended it; and to every place she brought suggestions and words of comfort and encouragement.

Nor was the zeal and energy of Madame Le Gras limited to the temporal wants of those among whom she went: in her way, and within her proper sphere, she cared for the souls as well as for the bodies of the poor; and so, while she remained in any place to look after the confraternities, she failed not, in whatever leisure time she could command, to collect the poor girls of the place in some house, where, with the sanction of the priest, she instructed them in the catechism and in their religious duties. And this was done with such meekness and true humility, that she won the hearts of all with whom she came in contact. If she found a school in the place, she cheerfully offered her assistance to the mistress, and spent the time working with her, really sharing in her labours, and not merely criticising what had been done; joining with her as a friend, and so winning her regard; while others might have destroyed all the good their skill would have done, by assuming the place of a superior, and making their very presence an act of condescension. If it happened that she found no school in the place, she would at once begin the work herself; gathering the children about her, she would enter, with all her ardent zeal and winning sweetness, into the wearisome task of laying the foundation upon which others were to build; and with untiring patience and never-failing gentleness she would gain the attention even of the most froward. Then would she select the best mistress she could find, and commit to her care the school she had begun.

For several years did she persevere in the arduous task thus committed to her, and far and wide extended the range of her influence; the dioceses of Beauvais, Paris, Senlis, Soissons, Meaux, Chalons in Champagne, and Chartres, witnessed her labours; village and city, highway and byway, alike shared her care; and wherever Vincent and his Priests of the Mission had been, and left their confraternities as memorials of their spiritual triumphs, her watchful eye examined the work, and her ready hand ministered to its needs. At her own cost the labour of love was fulfilled; and those who shared her toils, also shared the means which her piety provided for the journey. Thus did she, in company with other devout ladies, and attended by a servant, spend the greater portion of each year; and when winter forced them to return to Paris, she cared little for the rest her gentle frame and delicate health needed, but busied herself among the poor of the capital, and seemed to derive strength from the labours in which she so largely participated.

Vincent had designed these confraternities to supply, in some degree, the place of hospitals; and therefore he limited them at first to villages and hamlets, where no such institutions existed; but his old friend and zealous co-operator, the Bishop of Beauvais, seeing the spiritual good as well as temporal relief which they afforded, was unwilling to deprive his city of the blessing, and established them in each of its eighteen parishes. Not long afterwards, some pious ladies in Paris prevailed upon Vincent to found one in the parish of St. Saviour, in which they resided. This was in 1629, the year in which Madame Le Gras made her first visit to the confraternities; and upon her return to Paris, she called together some five or six of her neighbours, and united them with herself in the care of the poor of their parish. Vincent was at that time absent on the mission; but he quickly wrote, upon hearing from her respecting this good work, recommending that this new confraternity should follow the same rule as that already established at St. Saviour's, adding other suggestions fitted to their new sphere of action. The good which resulted from these new foundations speedily made itself known throughout Paris; and before the end of 1631 nearly every parish in the city and its suburbs had its confraternity.

For thirty years did Madame Le Gras continue her labour of love; in spite of bodily sufferings and many infirmities, she was enabled through so long a time to give herself entirely to the service of the poor, not only in the work we have just described, but in that renowned institution which sprang out of it; or which might perhaps be said rather to be its development and completion.

We have traced the beginnings of this great work, we have watched its early struggles, and the assistance it derived in its infancy from the gentle hand of this apostle of charity; let us now see it in the more perfect form it took when it grew up into the Order of the Sisters of Charity.

CHAPTER XIII.

THE SISTERS OF CHARITY.

THERE was an imperfection in these confraternities which speedily showed itself, and which confined very much their action. It was not that they failed to answer the end for which they were formed; but there was a narrow limit beyond which they could not reach, at least in their original shape. The rule required that each member should take her turn in watching and attending upon the sick; now as the confraternities extended and their numbers increased, it was found that many who became members could not spare the time required for the fulfilment of their duties; others, again, had no skill for such tasks; while some sent their servants to discharge these offices, which in their hands ceased to be a labour of love, and became so much work to be done, and that of no agreeable nature. It was soon evident, that if the duties undertaken were to be thoroughly performed, if the sick were to be constantly and duly tended, persons must be found who would give themselves entirely to the work; and who would not, like those who had other occupations, be called away from the sick-bed, and leave to less experienced hands the painful and arduous task.

The first remedy which suggested itself was the engagement of some female servants for this especial office; and Vincent remembered that on his missions he had frequently met with young women, who having no inclination for marriage, and yet having no vocation for the religious state, seemed just fitted for an employment in which they would have the protection which such a position afforded, and the freedom which those enjoy who are not bound by vows. He promised to bear this want in mind; and in the very next mission which he gave, he met with two such persons, whom he sent up to Paris, and placed in separate parishes, under the direction of the ladies of the confraternities of those places. These were afterwards followed by others, who were likewise placed severally in different parishes.

This arrangement did not prove very successful. In vain did Vincent direct, and Madame Le Gras advise them, as to how they should conduct themselves in respect to the ladies and the poor; there was no unity of action among them; they had had no previous training for the work; they did not understand it, and they did not like it. Actuated by no high principle, without the support and counsel which a community affords, they soon grew weary of their task, and gave as little satisfaction to others as to themselves. It was soon evident enough that this attempt would not succeed. Other motives besides pecuniary reward must uphold those who are to discharge such offices; something more than a wish to do one's duty is needful in the way of preparation. Vincent soon saw that a diligent and careful training was required; and, above all, that the exercises of a spiritual life were needed to strengthen those who would have so much to harass and distress them, living, as they would, in the constant presence of sickness and suffering. Nature would faint and grow weary under such trials; grace alone could conquer and persevere.

It now became clear what must be done, that the good work might be carried on effectually. Once more the ladies apply to Vincent to help them; and he, as usual, places the matter in the hands of God, and awaits patiently the result. It is not long before several young people present themselves for the work; and out of these the Saint selected four, and placed them under the control and instruction of Madame Le Gras.

It was in 1633 that the first attempt was made to deal systematically with the matter; and not without misgivings did Madame Le Gras enter upon the task she had undertaken. She could not but see the extreme difficulty of the work; while the comparative failures which had hitherto attended her efforts naturally made her most distrustful of this new attempt. However, come what might, the effort must be made; the want was too pressing to be put aside; the good to be gained was too great to be lost through lack of energy or perseverance. So she took heart, and began her work again with these four young girls; and what success followed all know. The little band grew into the "Sisters of Charity," a name as wide-spread as charity itself; dear to every Catholic heart, and respected even by those who are external to the Church; for does it not tell of self-denying love, of untiring zeal in the service of the sick and needy, of the truest and most perfect fulfilment of the Gospel precepts?

The success which crowned the efforts of Madame Le Gras quickly showed itself. The urgent demands of those about her drew forth her young pupils sooner than she could have wished; but such had been her zeal in the work, and so great the skill which directed it, that those whom she sent on the mission performed their tasks so well, gave such edification to those who saw them, and won such golden opinions from all sorts of men, that numbers desired to follow in their footsteps; and Madame Le Gras was overwhelmed with applications for admission to her house. Nor was their success to be wondered at, trained as they had been by one who understood the work so well. How skilful were they as nurses, how gentle and patient in bearing with the fretfulness and exactions of the sick, how exact in obeying the directions of physicians, how ready to sooth and console with the words of divine wisdom! No wonder that the sufferer grew calm in the presence of one so mild and tender as the Sister of Charity; no wonder that holy words told so effectually when they were enforced and illustrated by such charity and zeal. It was but natural that the physicians should proclaim their skill, that priests should commend their piety, and that the sick should esteem them as guardian-angels, and attribute their cure more to their care and ministrations than to all that science could achieve for them

It was the determination of Madame Le Gras not to limit the services of her community to any one parish or locality. Like the divine charity whose name they bore and whose precepts they fulfilled, they were scattered far and wide throughout the city; wherever they were most needed, there were they to be found; and none could know better than their superior where they could be most useful, for she it was who presided over all the confraternities of charity in the metropolis.

The growth of the institution was rapid beyond example. On every side there was a call for aid; and as fast as the sisters could be trained and sent out, others offered themselves to supply their places. During the life of Vincent de Paul not less than twenty-eight houses of the Sisters of Charity were founded in Paris alone; while far and wide the good work spread,— through the whole of France, into Lorraine, and even as far as Poland, where the zeal and charity of the queen planted and supported them. As time went on, and the order took firmer root, its charity embraced a wider range; and those who had at first limited their care and attention to the sick poor of different parishes, now took the widow and orphan under their charge, and neglected not the infirm and wounded soldier. Vincent gave them a fresh occupation when he intrusted to them the education of the foundlings and of poor young girls; and again, when he called them to the charge of several hospitals and of sick convicts. These varied occupations naturally divided the body into different congregations, each of which had its more especial task to fulfil; although they still continued under one general rule, with particular regulations suited for particular duties.

It was Vincent's practice to give at first only general directions to the bodies he organised; and when experience had tested these, to draw up fuller rules. It was so with his own order: the laws which governed it grew up from time to time, as occasion suggested and as necessity required; and so, after many years, when the formal code of rules was given by the Saint, it was found to contain little more than what was already in force. Every thing had thus been tested beforehand, and so, without anxiety or misgiving, he could bind his community to the observance of what had already answered so well and had the sanction of time and experience. The same course was pursued in respect to the Sisters of Charity: thus the institution existed for some years without a formal code of laws; but during the whole of that time the rule was growing up into full proportions. Without staying to examine in detail the general principles on which the institution was based, or the more precise rules by which they were carried out, it may be well to notice one or two of those chief points which Vincent was most anxious to impress upon all who were called to this difficult and arduous work.

They were never to lose sight of the one great end of their institution, which was, to honour and serve our Lord in the persons of the poor, the sick, the afflicted, and the unfortunate.

They were to render to these all the spiritual and corporal assistance in their power; and to do this most effectually, they were to sanctify themselves as much as possible, by uniting with outward acts of charity the interior exercises of a spiritual life.

He reminded them that they were not, and that they never could become Religious in the strict sense of the word; their employment forbade this. They were of necessity thrown into intercourse with the world; and if they would pass in safety through this severe ordeal, they must live as perfect a life as the most holy religious in their convents. To use the Saint's own touching language, "Their convent must be the houses of the sick, their cell the chamber of suffering, their chapel the parish-church, their cloister the streets of the city or the wards of hospitals; in place of the rule which binds nuns to the one enclosure, there must be the general vow of obedience, the grate through which they speak to others must be the fear of God, the veil which shuts out the world must be holy modesty."

They are to pass freely from place to place, and often must they be thrown into scenes of danger and temptation. What circumspection is needed amid such trials, what divine succour to guide and guard their steps! They are exhorted to live ever as in the immediate presence of God, and so to conduct themselves that the slightest whisper may never be breathed against them. No familiarities are to be permitted even among themselves; all childish and foolish sport or conversation is forbidden in recreation at home, and every precaution is to be redoubled when they go into the world on their mission of charity. Ere they set forth, they are to seek the divine protection at the foot of the Cross; and when they return, they are to give thanks for the mercy which watched over them.

Their life was to be one of self-denial and great strictness. They were to rise daily at four; twice a day they were to spend a considerable time in mental prayer; their food was to be the plainest, and wine was to be used only in cases of sickness. Each was to take her turn in watching the sick for a whole night, and to assist in the meanest and most repulsive offices. They must not shrink from infection, nor from scenes of misery and suffering; and when the hour of death should come, they were to assist their patients in their agony with the tenderest offices of charity.

Such was the rule two centuries ago; and such is it still. The holy discipline which trained the first Sisters of Charity under Madame Le Gras guides them now that they have spread from land to land, and the fruit of that discipline astonishes and delights all who come within its influence. The modern traveller notes it in his journal with as much wonder and admiration as those who, in Vincent's day, first witnessed its effects.

From time to time Vincent gave spiritual instructions to these young missionaries; and as they were frequently required to teach others, he called upon them to explain the Christian doctrine, and those matters which might be needed beside the bed of death, or which they had to instil into the youthful minds of those committed to their charge. And while the sisters, each in her turn, spoke as they were accustomed to do to the sick and dying, or adapted to the infant mind the great truths they had to convey, the heart of our Saint would warm with devotion, and his eyes would beam with delight, as he heard the words of truth fall so sweetly and with such touching eloquence from the lips of those whom he had so well prepared for their holy work.

Vincent had forbidden his order to undertake the spiritual direction of nuns; but he felt it right to make an exception, if such it can be called, in favour of the Sisters of Charity. The two orders were so closely united in the mission assigned to them, and in their common founder, that it seemed but natural that they should follow the same direction. Nevertheless, so careful was Vincent to avoid even the appearance of too close an intimacy, that he forbade the missionaries to visit the sisters without express permission, and carried out this rule most strictly in his own conduct, never seeing Madame Le Gras but upon some pressing necessity.

CHAPTER XIV.

THE HÔTEL-DIEU.

The name of Madame Le Gras does not stand alone in the annals of this great work of charity. Rank and beauty had another offering to make. There was one who amid the high circles of Paris occupied a prominent place, and whose beauty, talents, and wealth drew around her the great and noble. She was a young widow, graced with every attraction which could charm the eye and win the heart; and so, as might be naturally supposed, the hand of Madame la Présidente de Goussault was sought in marriage by many who could offer her the highest rank and the most brilliant position. But none of these could draw from a holier purpose the illustrious lady who had determined to leave a world which set so high a value on her, and to give herself and all she possessed to the service of God in His poor. She devoted herself to one especial task; and by her zeal she brought others round her, who, under her direction, carried into effect one of the noblest works of charity which Vincent ever undertook.

There was a large hospital at Paris, bearing the name of the Hôtel-Dieu, which, while it ministered to the temporal sufferings of the crowds within it, neglected sadly the spiritual maladies of its inmates. It seems to have had an efficient medical staff; but was poor enough in its array of chaplains. There was a pretence of spiritual care, which was, perhaps, worse than total neglect; for in the latter case there would have been not only an urgent call for a remedy, but an easy access to any who brought what was altogether wanting; but as matters stood, there was a difficulty in the way of introducing what seemed already provided for, while the fear of giving offence to those to whom was intrusted the spiritual charge, naturally deterred others from offering assistance which would appear to condemn the neglect which had made such assistance needful.

This hospital had attracted the especial attention of Madame de Goussault; she had frequently visited its extensive wards, her liberal hands had ministered to the wants of its suffering inmates, while her heart had as often grieved over the neglect with which their souls were treated. At length she addressed herself to Vincent; but so delicate did he feel the task to be, that for some time he resisted her earnest entreaties; and it was not until he had received the express command of the Archbishop, that he consented to take the matter in hand. Then, with the zealous co-operation of this noble lady, he set resolutely to work; and it was not long ere he had corrected the crying evil, and made that magnificent institution as perfect in its spiritual organisation as it had before been in its temporal arrangements.

Madame de Goussault invited some ladies of high rank to meet at her house, and to them Vincent addressed an earnest exhortation to take this enterprise in hand. On a subsequent day a second meeting was held, at which others attended; and the work was at once entered upon, Vincent becoming the director of the body. Ere long the attention of many ladies of the highest rank was drawn to their proceedings; and the contagion of good example spread so wide, that upwards of two hundred names of countesses, marchionesses, duchesses, and princesses were enrolled upon the list of those who took part in this labour of love, and who ministered with their own hands to the sick in the hospital. It was in 1634 that the work began. Their first care was to provide support and comfort beyond what the institution itself furnished; and this of itself must have been no small labour and expense, when we consider the multitudes who were received into the hospital: never less than a thousand beds were occupied, and sometimes the number was double. It was a fluctuating population; a large proportion left every day, whose places were as constantly supplied by fresh applicants: fifty, sixty, sometimes even a hundred would enter in a single day; and these would remain for eight or ten days, or perhaps for a month. Thus in a single year as many as twenty-five thousand would pass through its wards, some to the world again, and some to death. What a harvest of souls was here! what innumerable opportunities of calling sinners to repentance, of strengthening the weak, of healing and fortifying with blessed sacraments, and of preparing for death those who had neglected their religious duties! A holy instinct had led these pious ladies to this spot: we must now see how successfully they fulfilled the difficult mission to which they were called.

Vincent's prudence and skill were tried to the uttermost in obtaining admission for the ladies from the authorities of the hospital. It was true that he had the sanction of the Archbishop of Paris; but he well knew, that unless he could gain the good-will of those in power, the zeal and labour of the society would produce but little fruit. He therefore made it a point to put them under the constituted authorities, directing them, whenever they visited the hospital, to present themselves to the nuns who had the charge of it, and to offer their services to assist them, that they might have a share in their good works. He required them to treat these sisters with all possible respect and attention, and to obey them implicitly in all things; and when their services were not appreciated, they were to make excuses for the opposition they encountered, and never to annoy or oppose them. Acting upon these wise instructions, it was not long before all jealousy and ill-will disappeared. The nuns who had charge of the patients rejoiced at the assistance thus given them, and all combined in the same good work; the only emulation being that each endeavoured to excel the others in fulfilling her appointed task.

Their chief care was the comfort and consolation of the sick. From ward to ward, from bed to bed, the noble ladies passed, speaking in gentlest tones and in the most winning manner of the advantage of bearing sickness patiently, and of Him who watches over and cares for all. But they would not go empty-handed; the sufferings they witnessed, the many little wants they noticed, naturally led them to bring with them those small but highly-prized delicacies which the sick require. They soon found it necessary to systematise this relief, and they accordingly hired a room near the hospital, where they prepared what was most wanted. There they placed some of the Sisters of Charity, to dress the food, and to assist in the distribution of it. In this way they provided a morning meal of milk; but in time this was rendered unnecessary by the authorities undertaking to supply it. In the afternoon they brought some slight but nourishing refreshment, such as would tempt the appetite of the delicate, and bring a feeling of comfort to minds which, in so vast an establishment, must of necessity have felt lonely. Oranges, biscuits, jellies, and such-like things, if they did no other good, at least spoke of care and love, and of that sympathy which is more prized than all. And if such trifles as these served to open a heart which suffering and neglect had closed to holy influences, if they prepared the way for the word in season, who shall estimate their full value? He who despised not the cup of cold water given in His name and for His sake blessed these simple means, and poor sufferers learnt to lend a willing ear to those who thus showed a tender commiseration for their griefs. To those of their own sex the ladies had an especial mission; they instructed the ignorant, and prepared all for confession; they inspired them with good resolutions, whether for life or death.

In this difficult task Vincent was their guide. Lest they should seem to go beyond their province, and to usurp ecclesiastical functions, he prepared for them a book out of which they were to read the instructions they were to convey. They were not to preach, but to read. How careful he was to guard them against all danger and to remove whatever might be an impediment in their way, and how well he understood the influence of little things, appear as well from the rule just mentioned as from others he laid down for their guidance; as, for instance, when he requires these noble and high-born dames to dress themselves in all simplicity and plainness whenever they visited the hospital, to the end, as he says, "that if they come not as poor to the poor, they may at least lay aside all vanity and luxury of dress, so as not to give pain to the sick poor, who commonly feel their own wants most keenly in the presence of excess and superfluity." What deep knowledge of human nature is here, and what tenderest consideration for the afflicted! So, again, he exhorts them to use all affability and gentleness, lest an appearance of patronage and condescension should mar the good work. But they were too truly noble to fall into this error of little minds; they respected the poor, and honoured those who, in suffering at least, were like their Lord; and thus they fulfilled their holy mission, and did more than mere authority could do,—they won a ready obedience to their wishes, and were loved as much as they were respected.

About two years after the establishment of this society Vincent divided it into two parts; one of which devoted itself to the corporal wants of the sick, while the other occupied itself entirely with their spiritual needs. By this arrangement, each person had that work assigned to her for which she was best fitted, and two different offices were kept apart which it is so difficult to combine effectively. For three months the same ladies continued the work of visiting and instructing the sick daily; and then they resigned their office to others, giving at that time an account of what they had done, that those who succeeded them might profit by their experience. On these occasions Vincent would be present, and give such advice and directions as he thought needful. Of course the instructions given by the ladies could be but preparatory, and so priests were necessary to complete the work. To this end they engaged two chaplains; and as the duties soon became too arduous for so small a number, they increased this body to six, who were to devote themselves entirely to the care of the sick, in hearing the confessions of all, and in instructing the men. By this arrangement every one was duly prepared for making a general confession, whereas previously the practice had been to hear the confessions of the sick only at their first entrance into the hospital, when they were too generally but ill prepared; while it happened not unfrequently that heretics were brought in who, not liking to tell the truth, made sacrilegious confessions, and passed for Catholics. But now, under Vincent's rule and the care of these good ladies, things assumed a different appearance. Catholics were duly prepared for the sacraments; and heretics, impressed by what they saw around them, and moved by God's grace, declared their real state, consented to receive instruction, and in numberless cases were restored to the Church. In the very first year not less than 760 wanderers were thus brought home to the one fold.

The sum of money expended in the relief of the sick by these ladies was not less than 400*l*. a year. But great as is this amount, it sinks into insignificance when compared with the mighty work of charity they afterwards took in hand, when, under Vincent's direction, they ministered to the wants of whole provinces, and extended far and wide the succour which at first had been limited to the walls of the Hôtel-Dieu. In considering, however, this truly gigantic design, let us not forget, in our admiration of its splendour, the earlier but not less perfect work which owed its origin to the charity of these noble ladies, and which made the great hospital of Paris worthy of the name it bore. But before we speak of this great and extensive work, we must say something of an undertaking which preceded it in time, and which sprang up under the influence of Vincent's zeal, and was carried out by the devotion and energy of these same ladies.

CHAPTER XV.

THE FOUNDLING HOSPITAL.

THERE are few institutions in Paris which excite more admiration in strangers than the Foundling Asylum, the Hospice des Enfans trouvés, in the Rue d'Enfer. No one can visit it without being moved with feelings of love and veneration for St. Vincent de Paul, whose work it is; and when we call to mind the difficulties he had to encounter in first establishing it, and the still greater trials which threatened its very existence while it was yet young, we shall indeed acknowledge that it is His work who taught His servant to say, "When my father and mother forsook me, the Lord took me up."

Let us trace up this noble institution to its source in the charity of Vincent. Nothing could be more deplorable than the state of the poor foundlings of Paris when they first attracted the attention of our Saint. Not less than three or four hundred children were yearly left exposed by their parents in the public streets; and what does the reader think was the provision made by the government of that day for these little outcasts of society? It sounds well when we hear that a police-regulation required that every child thus found should be taken by certain officers to a house appointed for their reception; but if we follow these officers to La Couche, in the Rue St. Landry, what preparations do we find for the nurture and care of this crowd of helpless infants? A widow, with two or three servants; and these so miserably paid, that the barest necessities of life cannot be obtained for those who need the most delicate attention and care! There are no wet-nurses for the youngest, no fitting food for those who have been weaned. It naturally followed, that the greater part died almost immediately; while most of those who lingered on in a sickly existence were quieted in their pains, and in the end silenced for ever, by narcotics, which were given them by their ruthless guardians. Well was it for those who died thus; for they thereby escaped a harder and more cruel fate. Humanity shudders when it thinks of the lot of those who were given away, or sold for a few pence, to any who would take them from a place which it sounds like mockery to call their home. Some were hired to suck the milk from diseased breasts, who thus with their nurture drew in death; while others—horrible to relate—were bought as victims for diabolic art, and ministered with their blood to the requirements of those who sought therein restoration to health and a revival of the powers which sin and excess had corrupted and destroyed. The bath of infants' blood is no mere classic dream; for the seventeenth century saw revived (if they had ever really ceased) the mystic charms and satanic remedies which heathenism had used. And while the bodies of these little ones were thus neglected and suffered to perish, none cared for their souls. The miserable creature who had the nominal care of them herself confessed that she had never baptised one, nor did she know of a single case in which that blessed sacrament had been administered! And yet three or four hundred yearly entered her house.

This gigantic evil crossed Vincent's path: his tender heart recoiled in horror from cruelty so great and from neglect so terrible. To pass it with an exclamation of surprise or disgust, to drop over it a tear of sorrow, and thus to leave it, was not his way. His was an active charity, which shrank from no difficulty, and knew not the word "impossible." Yet was he prudent and cautious in what he undertook. He did nothing on impulse; and so he never gave up what he once began. Thus, in this case as in others, he considered long and carefully what he should do; he weighed his means against the requirements, and found that he must begin

in a small way. He called in the aid of the good ladies
of the Hôtel-Dieu, and sent them to examine the state
of "La Couche." They went, and saw what has been
related. What language could express their astonish
ment and distress at the spectacle which there presented itself! How can they meet so great a claim
upon their charity? how cope with so overwhelming
an evil? Under Vincent's advice, they agree to select
by lot twelve of these poor creatures, and place them
in a house near the gate of St. Victor. Madame Le Gras
and her Sisters of Charity undertook the immediate
charge of them, and wet-nurses were provided.

It was in 1638 that this first step was taken, and
gradually the number thus selected was augmented as
the means for their support increased; and the contrast
between those who had been thus taken and those who
were left behind moved the hearts of these generous
ladies to make greater sacrifices in their behalf. Thus
matters went on for two years; at the end of which
time, in 1640, Vincent called these ladies together, and
laid before them a design for completing the work by
taking charge of all these foundlings.

It was an arduous and costly task; and his prudence
would not suffer him to do more than urge them to make
trial of their strength and means. All he wished them
to do was to make an experiment. If their resources
would not suffice, they must give it up; in the meantime
he would try what he could do for them.

He was a man of business, and sat down to count
the cost of the enterprise; and this was the pecuniary
view of the case. The ladies had no more than 70*l.* of
fixed income which they could devote to this work: at
Vincent's request, the queen regent, Anne of Austria, ever
forward in works of charity, gave an annual grant of
600*l.*; and to this our Saint added all that he could spare
from the resources of St. Lazarus and from the funds which
the charitable placed at his disposal. After all, there was
a large additional sum required to meet the necessary expenditure, which was certainly not less than 2,000*l.* a year.

Nobly did they struggle on against all difficulties for
some years; every nerve seemed strained, every power
taxed to the uttermost, to carry on the undertaking
and to preserve the poor deserted ones from the fate
which awaited them should they have to return to their
old quarters. But now difficulties increase: national
distress shows itself on all sides, the curse of faction
once more comes over the land, sin and misery rise together in greater force than ever; and so the demands
upon this especial charity augment with its increasing
poverty. Moreover, the famine which at this time afflicted the province of Lorraine called for unexampled
relief; and those who had burdened themselves with the
charge of the foundlings are now foremost in aiding the
efforts which Vincent is making for the support of thousands of their starving countrymen.

Can we wonder if at such a time the hearts of these
noble women should despond, and that their resolution
respecting the orphans should falter? Common prudence seemed to urge them to consolidate their energies
on the more pressing need, and to give up, at least for
a time, what, after all, had been undertaken only as
an experiment. Such was the state of affairs in 1648,
when Vincent took his resolution, and called once more
around him those liberal souls who were doing so
much.

The general meeting is held; Vincent is there, and
in the crowd of those present we may observe Madame
Le Gras, as well as Madame de Goussault. Every heart
beats high with anxiety—for what will Vincent advise?
He is so cautious, so prudent, that, it may be, the more
enthusiastic are half-inclined to condemn his counsel
beforehand; while those who have more calmly weighed
the matter in hand sigh as they feel the necessity of
drawing back from what seems a hopeless task. At
any rate there is this consolation, that they have done
their best; and that, had not these national calamities
come so unexpectedly upon them, they might still have
persevered. It is painful, indeed, to draw back; but is

it not madness to go on? Thus they thought; and therefore their hearts were sad, and many a bright eye was dimmed with tears for those whom they were about to abandon.

But what thinks Vincent all this while? It may be that their own thoughts occupy them too exclusively, or those ladies might have marked a determination about the Saint's brow, and a sweet expression of ardent charity in those benignant eyes, which would in part have revealed the purpose within his mind.

And now Vincent rises; and in breathless silence they listen to the words of their sage counsellor, while he weighs the momentous question, whether they shall continue or give up the charge of the poor foundlings. Calmly and impartially does he set forth the reasons on both sides. He reminds them that it is only an experiment they have been making, and that consequently they are not bound by any obligation to continue it. But then he fails not also to call to their remembrance the fruit of their labours; how five or six hundred infants have been snatched from the hands of death, many of whom have learnt, and others were now being taught trades, by means of which they cease to be an expense to any one. He then goes on to tell them how through their care these little ones have been brought to know and to serve God; how with their earliest accents they have learned to speak of Him; and what bright hopes for a happy future these good beginnings presage. As he speaks, his words grow warmer; and at last, with deep emotion, and with irresistible sweetness, he exclaims: "Yes, ladies, compassion and charity have led you to adopt these little creatures for your children; you became their mothers by grace, when those who are their mothers by nature abandoned them; see now, if you too will forsake them. Cease to be their mothers, that you may become their judges; their life and death are in your hands. I have now to receive your decision. The time has come for you to pronounce sentence, and to declare whether or no you will still have pity on them. If you continue your charitable care over them, they will live; if you abandon them, they will undoubtedly perish. Your own experience forbids you to doubt it."

The result may be easily imagined. Cost what it might, the good work should go on; and with tearful eyes but joyful hearts, they resolved to take courage from the words of Vincent, and to persevere in what was so evidently the will of God.

The king granted them the chateau at Bicêtre, which Louis XIII. had destined for invalided soldiers; and thither for a time they sent the infants who had been weaned; but the air proving too keen, they were soon brought back to Paris, and lodged in a house near St. Lazarus. Here they were intrusted to twelve Sisters of Charity, who brought them up, and communicated to them the first rudiments of education. Those who were not yet weaned were given in charge to some country women, and were visited from time to time by the sisters, and occasionally by the Fathers of the Mission.

In course of time two houses were bought for these children. Louis XIV. increased the annual grant which his mother had made; and the good queen-dowager continued throughout her life the patronage she had so generously extended to the charity in the hour of its greatest need. From that day to this the institution has flourished; and those who visit it in its present habitation in the Rue d'Enfer, or in any other of its many dwelling-places, find as of old the Sisters of Charity carrying on the very work Vincent left in their hands, and recognise in its vitality another token of the heavenly mission of him whose works not only remain in vigorous life to the present day, but grow and expand with the wants and necessities of each succeeding age.

CHAPTER XVI.

CONVICTS, IDIOTS, AND REPROBATES.

There was one class among the suffering poor which seemed to have an especial attraction for the heart of Vincent; perhaps it was their utter friendlessness which drew him towards them. They had so long been neglected, that no one cared for their souls; and the charity which sought its objects on every side passed them by as though it recognised them not, or as though its influences had no power to move them. The poor convicts won Vincent's early love, and to the last he clung to them.

We have already seen what he did to improve their condition at Marseilles, when, in company with his good friend and patron, the Count de Joigny, he went among them, and by his untiring zeal and fervent charity roused them from their sinful apathy, and opened their hardened hearts to the gentle influences of religion. We marked, too, how on his return to Paris he engaged a house near the church of St. Roch, and removed the poor creatures from their loathsome dungeons to this more fitting place of detention. Years have passed away since then; but all this time Vincent's care has watched over them; his hands have ministered to their needs, and his spiritual direction has guided many among them into better ways. And now, after thirteen years, he seeks to perpetuate the work which ere long he must commit to others, and to fix it upon a firmer footing than that which has hitherto served his purpose. The house near St. Roch is, after all, but a hired building, upon which his hold is very uncertain. There is an ancient tower which stands between the river and the gate of St. Bernard; it is one of those

vast edifices which seem built to resist the ravages alike
of man and time, and which, when they have served
their immediate purpose, remain as landmarks to tell of
what has been, and rear their worn fronts like beings of
a past age, dark, silent, and alone. This deserted tower
will answer Vincent's purpose well; here, at any rate,
he will be secure from molestation; so, having obtained
it as a gift from Louis XIII., he fits it up, and places
in it these poor criminals. The year 1632, which saw
the Fathers of the Mission enter into their new home
at St. Lazarus, witnessed also the removal of the convicts to this more commodious dwelling.

For seven years the heavy charge of the work
rested on Vincent; for the government seemed to content itself with sanctioning what he did, and with
granting him the building in which his care and vigil-
ance were to be exercised. In Madame Le Gras, however, he found a zealous and active assistant. The old
tower, indeed, was in her parish; and so, without
going out of her way, she could divert a portion of the
funds and attentions of her charitable association to the
requirements of the convicts. Yet, after all, the demands of such an establishment pressed so heavily
upon the young institution of St. Lazarus, that, had not
God raised up an unlooked-for benefactor, the burden
might have been greater than it could have safely
borne.

It was about this time that a certain rich lady died,
who left by will an annual charge upon her estate of
300*l*., to be applied by her daughter and heiress, under
the advice of some ecclesiastic, to the relief of criminals
condemned to the galleys. Vincent, upon hearing of
this legacy, naturally applied to the family for what
was so evidently intended for the work in which he was
engaged; but he had to encounter many difficulties on
the part of the husband of the heiress, and it was only
by the intervention of the procurator-general, M. Molé,
that he could induce him to join with his wife in the
investment of a sufficient sum of money out of the estate

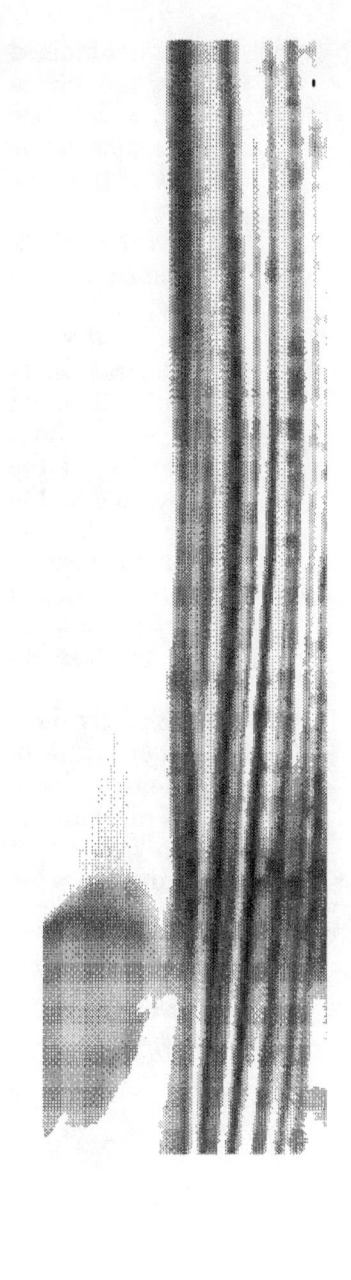

ing obtained
, and places
, which saw
r new home
l of the con-

of the work
emed to con-
d, and with
re and vigil-
e Gras, how-
nt. The old
so, without
ortion of the
ciation to the
r all, the de-
d so heavily
that, had not
r, the burden
have safely

rich lady died,
her estate of
heiress, under
ef of criminals
on hearing of
mily for what
which he wa
difficulties
nd it was
neral, M.
his wife
ut of th

to produce this annual income. It seems, however, that the objection was merely of a technical character; for when Vincent had an opportunity of explaining what the state of the convicts had been before he had taken their cause in hand, and the beneficial effects of his labours among them, these good people willingly co-operated with him, and only stipulated that some portion of the income should be paid to the Sisters of Charity whom Vincent had determined to send among them. The priests of the parish were also to be paid for saying Mass and giving regular instructions, and Vincent reserved to himself the privilege of giving them missions from time to time, especially when their numbers were greater than usual, and when the time came for any to be sent to the galleys at Marseilles.

Thus were these poor outcasts cared for and tended during their stay in Paris, and no longer left to pine in an atmosphere laden with moral poison, where sin daily grew stronger in souls which had fallen, and where what remained of good died out and perished. Vincent's care had provided a prison where correction went hand in hand with amendment, and the penalty which the violated law enforced became an instrument for the salvation of souls.

But not content with what he had done for them in Paris, his love for these convicts followed them to the galleys, and there, where Vincent had first learned their sorrows and sufferings, he once more toils for their temporal and spiritual welfare. His friend, the Count de Joigny, is no longer general of the galleys, for he has passed to his eternal reward; but there is one now filling that office who is as willing as he to listen to Vincent's advice, and whose power far surpasses that which even a De Gondi wielded. The great cardinal who sought the counsel of Vincent in matters of moment, and who never turned his ear from the frank speech of one he so esteemed, is as ready as ever to assist him in a good work; and when Richelieu takes a matter in hand, there is little chance of its failing for lack of energy or means to carry it through. It sounds like figurative language, and yet it is literally true, to say that Cardinal Richelieu built upon the foundation which Emmanuel de Gondi laid. The hospital which Vincent found so needful at Marseilles De Gondi began to build; but the troubles of those distracted times stayed the work, and so it was reserved for his successor, Richelieu, to complete what the former had so well begun. It is pleasing to couple in this noble enterprise another name which sheds a gentle lustre over a scene so fair, and to record that the cardinal's niece, the Duchess d'Aiguillon, gave no less a sum than 700*l.* to support four priests of Vincent's congregation, who were to devote themselves entirely to the care of the convicts and to give missions to those who were placed in different parts of the kingdom. In due time the hospital thus built was endowed by Louis XIV. with an income of 600*l*., and grew up into a very flourishing institution; and that monarch, at the suggestion of his mother, the regent, Anne of Austria, confirmed Vincent in his office of royal chaplain to the galleys; and to mark his esteem for the Congregation of the Fathers of the Mission, decreed that the superior of that body should ever hold that chaplaincy which Vincent so worthily filled.

It was in the year 1622, according to his biographer Collet, that Vincent, paying a visit incognito to the galleys at Marseilles, offered himself in the place of a convict, more unfortunate than criminal, whom he found piteously bewailing the ruin he had brought upon his wife and children by his misconduct. The exchange was made; and for several weeks, until he was recognised, Vincent wore the fetters and endured all the hardships of a galley-slave. The authenticity of this heroic act of self-sacrifice has, indeed, been brought into question; but a modern historian[*] declares that the fact is attested by the superior of the Fathers of the Mission who were established at Marseilles in the year 1643, and is further corroborated by an old manuscript left by

[*] Rohrbacher, *Histoire de l'Eglise*, vol. xxv. p. 323.

the Sieur Dominique Beyrie, a relative of the Saint. It is related also that one of his priests once asked Vincent if the story were true, and whether the swelling in his ancles, from which he suffered, was not owing to the chains he wore at that time; to which the Saint only replied by smiling and turning the conversation.

It may not be out of place to notice here two works which Vincent carried on at St. Lazarus, and from which no duties, however urgent, could divert him.

We mentioned before, that when Vincent first came to the Priory of St. Lazarus, he found there some poor idiots whom the charity of the prior, M. Le Bon, was supporting: these immediately became the object of our Saint's especial care; he would let none deprive him of an exercise of purest charity, of that charity which seeks no return, but finds its reward in itself. Nor did he limit his care to those whom he found already in the house; he rejected none that were brought to him, but found great consolation, in the midst of many cares and anxieties, in the humbling offices which such a charge involved.

But there was another class of beings whom he received into the priory, far more difficult to manage, and far more dangerous members of society. Many a young person came under Vincent's care whose case was more desperate than that of the poor idiots. Those who had plunged themselves into vice and dissipation, who had turned a deaf ear to the remonstrances of friends and kindred, and whom no other mode of correction could reach, were sent by their distressed relatives to the priory, that under the instruction and guidance of Vincent they might have one more chance of returning to a sense of duty and recovering the position of which their vices had deprived them. Thus St. Lazarus became a hospital for spiritual lepers.

The evil to be overcome was great; and the remedy, though apparently severe, was admirably adapted for its purpose. There was a mystery and abruptness about it which told upon those whom milder courses would

have failed to impress; and as it was done with the
sanction of lawful authority, there was no danger of
its abuse, even in less careful hands than those of Vincent. The young reprobate, upon whom all reproof and
exhortation seemed to have been thrown away, and
who was daily sinking deeper and deeper into sin, was
suddenly snatched away from his evil companions and
carried off in the silence of the night to the Priory of
St. Lazarus. Upon his arrival he was conveyed to a
solitary chamber, none but the Superior knowing his
name and rank; and there, while all due care was taken
of him, he was left to commune alone with his own
conscience. The sudden capture, the loss of those upon
whose society he had hitherto been dependent, the
stillness and solitude of the place, all conspired to
fill his mind with a sense of awe, mingled perhaps for
a time with a feeling of indignation. At first little
could be done beyond the benefit which every mind
must derive from being thrown back upon itself; but
as time passed on, opportunities would present themselves, which Vincent knew so well how to use, for sage
counsel and affectionate influence to do their work upon
the sinner. The calm which succeeds the storm of
passion leaves the heart open to the influx of better
feelings; and the hollowness of worldly joys, especially
when they have been polluted by sinful indulgence,
never forces itself more convincingly upon the mind
than when those pleasures have suddenly passed away,
and left behind only the sting of a troubled conscience.
The poor prodigal began to yearn after the inward peace
to which he had so long been a stranger, to abhor the
evil over which the fascinations of society had thrown
a fatal disguise, and to turn a willing ear to the holy
men who so gently and lovingly ministered to his wants,
and whose only aim was the salvation of his soul.
Surely there is contagion in virtue as well as in vice!
Brought thus under the daily action of purer and better
influences, his mind, tranquillised by the peace and
quiet of this holy retreat, became more accessible to

the attractions and solicitations of grace. By and by
the gardens were thrown open to the penitent, and he
could walk at large and enjoy the freshness of the
balmy air and the beauty of the flowers, themselves the
symbols of that purity and innocence, the love of which,
now that he was removed from the enthralling temptations of the world, had begun to revive in his heart.
Thus all combined to develop aspirations after good,
and to awaken in him a desire of reconciliation with
God and peace with his own conscience. And now,
his pride subdued, his heart softened, and his hopes of
mercy re-animated, it was not long before he cast himself in contrition at the feet of his spiritual father, and
unburdened himself of his tale of guilt and sorrow; and
so when, after being carefully watched and tended
during his convalescence, and fortified by all those spiritual aids which Vincent knew so well how to apply
for the restoration of the repentant sinner, he went forth
once more into the world, he was no longer the weak
thing of former days, swayed by every evil influence
and the slave of each unruly passion; but, strong in the
grace of holy sacraments, and resolute in the course he
had set before him, he returned to those dear relatives
who once despaired of his recovery, and gave to the
world another example of the many blessings which
Vincent was every day conferring upon mankind. Many
a broken heart has been healed by the return to life of
one who seemed worse than dead, many a sinking family
has been upheld by the reform of its reprobate head,
and many a man who has risen to honour and renown
has owed all the world has given, and far more than
the world can give, to the zeal of the holy Fathers who,
under the guidance of Vincent, gave themselves to this
work of spiritual healing.

CHAPTER XVII.

LORRAINE—ITS SUFFERINGS AND ITS SUCCOURS.

WE must now for a time withdraw our eyes from what might be called the domestic scenes among which we have found ourselves, and look abroad upon the noisy and tumultuous world which lies beyond. The quiet of St. Lazarus must be left behind, and we must travel through a war-distracted and desolate land, to a scene of misery and suffering which perhaps has not its parallel in history.

Paris had grown wearied with the cries of agony which were for ever resounding from all sides; year after year the same dismal note of wailing had been heard from a people worn out by war and famine, until at last men began to disregard what had grown almost into the established order of things, and to look upon it as a necessary evil. But suddenly there is a louder cry, which startles even the dullest from their apathy; for it tells of suffering almost beyond belief, and reveals a depth of degradation and horror from which the stoutest heart recoils. That cry is from Lorraine; it smites on Vincent's ear, and at once he is up and listening to catch the import of the sound.

But, in order that we may understand the nature and cause of the distress which roused our Saint to the gigantic efforts which we are about to describe, it is necessary to look back a little into the history of the period which preceded this year of suffering, 1639.

The thirty years' war was still raging; that desolating war which, as Schiller says, "from the interior of Bohemia to the mouth of the Scheldt, and from the banks of the Po to the coasts of the Baltic, devastated whole countries, destroyed harvests, and reduced towns and villages to ashes; which opened a grave for many thousand combatants, and for half a century smothered the glimmering sparks of civilisation in Germany, and threw back the improving manners of the country into their pristine barbarity and wildness."

Most of the great actors in that terrible tragedy had passed from the scene, and the battles which have left a name in history had nearly all been fought; yet the end had not yet come. Wallenstein had risen like a meteor in that murky atmosphere; his course of mingled triumph and disgrace had been run; his deeds of greatness and of sin had been performed, and he had fallen by the hand of an assassin when his treason was at its worst. Gustavus Adolphus, too, had passed away. Leipsic had witnessed his triumph over Tilly, and Lutzen saw his death in the hour of victory; yet still the war raged fiercely. From land to land it passed; and wherever it came it brought ruin and desolation. Like a tempestuous sea, it swallowed up all that came within its power; its waves rolled on; and where plenty had been, famine and despair alone remained.

Among the many countries which were thus ravaged, there was not one which suffered so severely as the little kingdom of Lorraine. But a few years before it had been overrun by the French armies, on the ground, among other political reasons, of its duke having broken his promised neutrality and joined the imperialists in defence of Catholic Germany. Unable to remain an indifferent spectator of the great contest between the Catholic head of the empire and the heretical Swede, he had thrown himself with less prudence than courage in the way of Gustavus Adolphus, flushed with his victory just gained at Leipzic. Gustavus swept the duke's army before him with the power and rapidity of a torrent; and the defeated prince returned in haste to his country only to find it a prey to the French invaders. France finally seized on Lorraine; and now, when its legitimate sovereign is endeavouring to obtain re-possession of his dominions, the unhappy country, just recovering from the effects of the former invasion, again becomes the theatre of war, and of the fierce ravages of Duke Bernard of Weimar, who rushes down on its fair plains and carries fire and sword throughout the kingdom. Religious animosity inflamed the bad passions which already burned with so much fury; and all things, sacred and common, were alike destroyed. Terrible is the picture which contemporary writers draw of this invasion; there was no safety for nuns in convents, for travellers on the road, for cattle in the pastures, or for labourers in the fields. Many towns and villages were entirely depopulated; others were reduced to ashes; famine and pestilence attacked what remained of the people; and such was the state of desolation, that wolves came from the forests and penetrated into the very streets, where they devoured the bodies of those who had none to bury them, and even attacked women and children. Calmet has told the hideous tale in language forcible from its very simplicity. "The country-people," he says, "livid and gaunt through famine, fought for the very grass, the roots of trees and acorns, and devoured ravenously the most putrid carrion. At last famine brought them to such a state, that men killed one another for food. A man dared not sleep beside his neighbour, lest his throat should be cut during the night; one mother made a compact with another, that they should share the body of her child, on condition that the second should give up her infant for the same horrible purpose on a future day; a brother fiercely attacked his sister to tear from her the bread she was eating; and children killed their parents, and fought among themselves for their mangled limbs."

Well might Father Caussin, the king's confessor, exclaim, when the report of these awful deeds and sufferings reached his ears, "*Sola Lotharingia Hierosolymam calamitate vincit*—Lorraine alone surpasses Jerusalem in suffering." Terrible as were the miseries which afflicted the holy city when it was besieged by Titus, they were exceeded by those which visited Lorraine, when Christian rose against Christian, and the foulest deeds were perpetrated in the name of religion.

Such was the misery which afflicted Lorraine, and which cried aloud for help. Vincent heard that cry, and at once responded to its appeal. He called his congregation together, and advised them to set an example worthy of the occasion, and to show to others how self-denying is real charity. But what could they do? What superfluities had they to cut off, what luxuries to abandon, that with the money thus saved they might have wherewithal to help the starving people of Lorraine? He gave all the money they had in the house to this purpose; but this was not enough to satisfy his ardent charity. He could not do much in the way of retrenchment; for already had their ordinary simple fare been diminished when the troubles of 1636 had driven so many poor creatures from the country into Paris. But still something must be done; and so he substituted rye-bread for wheaten, and reduced one half their portion of wine. "These are times of penance," said he; "for God is afflicting His people. Is it not, then, our office to be at the foot of the altar, mourning the sins of others? To so much we are bound by obligation; but ought we not moreover to retrench something of our daily fare for the relief of others?" And not one of the Fathers raised a murmur; for he who spoke thus was the first to practise what he enjoined.

And now that he had made a beginning at home, Vincent could with a better grace call others to his aid in this great enterprise. His first appeal was to Madame de Goussault and the ladies over whom she presided, and, as he expected, they entered readily and heartily into his plans. But the want was greater than he and they could meet, for it affected a whole kingdom and every class within its limits. What of that? Should Vincent's heart fail him because the task was heavy, and should he doubt of success because exertion and toil were needed in its prosecution? Men of less faith might have shrunk from so gigantic a labour; but it was a characteristic of our Saint to rise with the occasion, and to draw courage from what daunted others.

His ordinary resources were soon exhausted, and then he had recourse to others. Fortunately for Lorraine, there were those whose means were as ample as their dispositions were generous, to whom Vincent never applied for help in vain. The Duchess d'Aiguillon, the niece of Cardinal Richelieu and heiress of his great wealth, used with no sparing hand the power and means which her exalted position placed at her disposal; and he who stood so high in the good opinion of the all-powerful uncle exercised no less an influence over the noble-minded and generous niece. The duchess responded warmly to the appeal of Vincent; and thus the charity which flowed towards Lorraine widened its channel and grew more commensurate with the need which called it forth.

But there was another, in still higher place, to whom our Saint made known the want of Lorraine, and from whom he received no slight assistance. This was no less a person than the queen herself, Anne of Austria. Not long before the time of which we are writing, she had given birth to a son, who in a very few years became Louis XIV.; and now she seems anxious to show her gratitude for this long-wished-for blessing by casting with a lavish hand her charities into Vincent's treasury. Thus aided on all sides, our Saint has means almost equal to the appalling necessities to which he had undertaken to minister; and Lorraine experiences what the burning charity of one man could do in relieving what had lately been an independent kingdom, and was now one of the chief provinces of France.

We may judge of the wants which came before him, when we find that he kept from starvation for several long years not fewer than five-and-twenty towns; that he had moreover to succour crowds of country-people, as well as priests, and religious of both

sexes; that the sick and wounded were thrown upon his
hands; and that such was the distress which sought his
aid, that he had literally to clothe the naked as well as
feed the hungry, his agents finding to their horror whole
multitudes of people without a single rag to cover them.
It was Vincent's part not only to arouse the charity of
the faithful and to collect the alms, but to organise a
plan for their distribution This was a task for which
he was especially fitted. With the most ardent zeal
and the most untiring energy, which recognised obstacles only to overcome them, he combined that common
sense and those business-like habits which qualified
him for the arrangement of the smallest details as well
as for undertaking the most extensive operations. His
first care was to send into different parts of Lorraine
a dozen of his missionaries, and some of the Fathers
of the congregation who were skilled in medicine and
surgery. He gave them full and complete rules for
their guidance, and especially enjoined upon them the
necessity of taking no important step without first consulting the ecclesiastical authorities of the place. By
these means he protected his agents from even the appearance of unauthorised interference, and gained for
them the countenance and support of the local clergy.
The first town in which this relief was given was Toul,
where the congregation had a house of their own; and
from their labours there, we may judge of the zeal and
energy with which this duty was fulfilled in other parts
of Lorraine. There is still preserved a document, dated
December 20th, 1639, written by the vicar-general,
Jean Midot, who administered the diocese during the
vacancy of that see, in which he states, that for two
years these priests clothed and fed a crowd of poor
people, whom they also supplied with medicines; that
they received sixty patients into their house, and supported a hundred in the suburbs, besides giving their
services to the wounded in the royal army. Nor was
this the only testimonial from Toul; for the Dominican-
esses, who had two convents in that place, bear grate-

ful testimony, not only to the services rendered to the wounded soldiers, but to the support which, for two years and a half, they themselves received, and to which, indeed, they owed their preservation from starvation. "Blessed be God," they conclude, "who has sent us these angels of peace, in a time of such calamities, for the good of this city, for the consolation of His people, and for our own in particular."

Vincent discouraged the sending of such documents as these, and only permitted an account to be forwarded of the money expended, that he might satisfy all parties as to the use that had been made of their alms.

Perhaps, of all places in Lorraine, the city of Metz suffered most severely. Not less than four or five thousand of its inhabitants wandered about the streets in the utter helplessness of distress. Not a morning came but showed some ten or twelve dead bodies of those who had perished of want during the night, and hideous tales were whispered about of those whose misery had been suddenly cut short by the attack of wolves. Would that this were the worst! alas, famine destroyed souls as well as bodies; and there were wretched creatures who, to preserve life, sold that which should be dearer than life, and bartered away their womanly honour for a morsel of bread. Nay, a danger threatened, which seemed, if possible, still more fearful; for several religious communities of women were on the point of abandoning their cloisters, and casting themselves on the world, in those evil days when scarce the cloister could protect their innocence from the violence of a licentious soldiery.

Miserable indeed was the spiritual and temporal state of Metz. In the previous year (1638) the parliament had deserted it for Toul, and carried with it what little succour its presence might have afforded; while the extent of its spiritual destitution may be measured by the simple fact, that its bishop, a natural son of Henry IV., had never even received orders, and left his people to die of famine, while he squandered at court the income of his diocese and of six rich abbeys which he also enjoyed!

Verdun, another of its chief cities, had little to boast over its miserable neighbour. Its bishop had taken an active part in the wars which desolated the kingdom; and now that Lorraine had passed under the rule of France, he vainly opposed the authority of Louis, and in the ardour of his zeal excommunicated all those citizens who assisted in the restoration of the citadel. Obliged to fly from his diocese, he betook himself to Cologne, where he collected a body of troops, and returned to besiege Verdun, with no other result than an increase of misery to his poor subjects. For three years did the missionaries remain in that city, during which time they continued to distribute bread among from four to six hundred poor starving creatures; they provided meal and soup for sixty sick people, to whom money was also freely given. Nor did their charity stop here: no less than thirty persons of better condition received private relief from them; while at all hours of the day bread was given to crowds of poor people who came in for relief from the country, and clothing was freely distributed among them all.

It is scarcely necessary to add, that Vincent's love of souls was not idle in these ministrations for the body. The season of calamity is frequently one of great spiritual graces. Vincent's lessons had not been lost on his children; he spoke by their lips; his love beamed in their eyes; his charity burned in their hearts. Thus was Verdun filled with sights at which there is joy in heaven: patient resignation in extreme distress; love of God when affliction was heaviest; souls saved while bodies perished; penitents reconciled; sinners converted; and those who in prosperity had neglected their chief duties brought by adversity to their Father's house. Well might one of those missionaries exclaim, in a letter to Vincent, "How many souls are brought to heaven by poverty! Since I have been in Lorraine, I have assisted more than a thousand poor people at the hour of death, all of whom appeared to be well prepared. See, then, how many intercessors there are in heaven for those who have assisted them on earth." Without dwelling upon the details of similar scenes in other parts of Lorraine, we may mention, that in Nancy the able-bodied were supported by alms; and as there was no work in which they could be employed, the opportunity was taken to give them a mission, which was so successful, that the greater portion of them, about five hundred, became regular monthly communicants. As for the sick, the missionaries placed as many as possible in the public hospital, where they provided them with what was needful; and the rest they received into their own house. They made a daily distribution to a hundred aged and infirm poor, who were lodged in different parts of the city, and took especial care of women who were nursing infants.

At Bar-le-Duc the missionaries were received and lodged by the Jesuit Fathers, who shared their labours with them. Here the distress was as great as at Nancy and Verdun; and the same energy and self-denial were displayed in relieving it. A terrible disease increased the sufferings of the people, whose compunction and penitence equalled their misery and distress. Crowds besieged the confessionals; and one at least of the missionaries fell an early victim to his zeal and devotion. Germain de Montevil was but twenty-eight years of age when he arrived at Bar-le-Duc, and in one month he heard upwards of eight hundred general confessions. He sank under the effort, and was buried by the Jesuits in their college-chapel, followed to the grave by a crowd of poor, who "wept," an eye-witness relates, "as if they had lost a father."

At Pont-à-Mousson the missionaries witnessed a scene of terrible suffering. They brought relief to those who were too exhausted to receive it; hundreds of gaunt beings, with scarcely the aspect of men, stretched forth their hands for food, and died in the effort to eat it! Women and children dared not walk the streets, in which the wolves prowled at large; and assistance had to be taken to their houses, to which they were confined through fear of these fierce animals, or, it may be, of beings still more fierce and savage, who, human in name and form, had lost through suffering their human nature, and madly devoured their fellow-creatures. Terrible as this picture is, it is not overdrawn; for there is a formal document of that date which tells the almost incredible story of a child murdered, torn in pieces, and devoured by children but little older than himself!

The sufferings of the time had fallen heavily upon every class, and not the least severely upon the clergy. Several among them had perished with their flocks; and the consequence was, that many places were without priests, and children died in great numbers without baptism. To meet this pressing evil, which could not be relieved by those who already were overburdened with the work to which Vincent had sent them, our Saint engaged two other priests to traverse the diocese of Toul, to baptise all who had not as yet received that sacrament, and also to instruct fit persons in each canton in the manner of administering the same, that children who should be afterwards born might receive baptism at their hands.

Thus every need, spiritual and temporal alike, became the care of Vincent; and to each his ready hand extended the remedy which his thoughtful mind devised.

At St. Mihiel there was an aggravation to the distress which that place shared with the rest of Lorraine; for the opposition which Richelieu had there met with had induced him to send a French garrison into the town. We cannot give a better idea of the sufferings which Vincent's missionaries discovered than is conveyed in a letter from one of those ministers of charity. "I began," he writes, "as soon as I arrived, to distribute alms; but I found so vast a number of poor, that I knew not how to relieve all. There are more than three hundred of them in great distress, and as many others who are reduced to the utmost extremity. I tell you the truth, sir, there are more than a hundred of them mere living skeletons; so frightful to behold, that if our Lord did not strengthen me, I could not endure the sight of them. Their skin is like marble, and so shrunk, that their teeth stand out dry and exposed; their eyes and faces are quite withered; in short, it is the most terrible scene that can be imagined. They dig up roots in the fields, which they dress and eat. I wish especially to recommend these great calamities to the prayers of the company. There are several ladies of noble birth who are perishing with hunger, and among them some who are young. I am in dread lest despair should drive them to wretchedness worse than death." Another letter from this same priest informs Vincent that he has distributed bread to eleven hundred and thirty-two poor creatures, without including the many sick whom he had assisted. It also bears ample testimony to the patience with which these sufferings were borne, and to the gratitude which found its vent in prayers for their benefactors.

Vincent was anxious to know the full particulars of the miseries with which he had undertaken to deal. To this end he determined upon sending one of his first companions to visit the different places in which he had placed his agents. He had another object also in view, which was, to see how the work of relief was being carried on, and how far those he had sent were exercising fitting prudence and discretion in its execution. It was his duty as superior to watch over those who had put themselves under his rule, and to prevent their undertaking labours beyond their strength.

The report of this priest is full of interest; but we must content ourselves with one extract, and it shall be one which relates to this same St. Mihiel:

"I will tell you, sir, of things which have occurred in this place, and which are so extraordinary, that had we not seen them with our own eyes, we should not have believed them. Besides the poor mendicants I have already mentioned, the greater part of the inhabitants, and especially the highest class, endure such extremes of hunger as can be neither described nor imagined; and what makes this still more deplorable is, that they have not the face to beg. There are some among them, it is true, who conquer this sense of shame; but others will rather die; and I have myself spoken to some persons of condition who do nothing but weep at such a state of things. Here is another fact still stranger: a widow woman, having no food left for herself and her three children, and seeing nothing before them but starvation, skinned a snake, and laid it on the fire to roast for food. Our brother who resides in this place heard of it, and hastened to the spot; he witnessed the fact I have related, and administered proper relief. If a horse dies in the town, no matter of what disease, it is at once seized upon and devoured; and not more than three or four days ago a woman was found at the public place where relief is distributed, who had a lap full of putrid flesh, which she was giving to other poor people in exchange for morsels of bread. Another very deplorable circumstance is, that the priests, who are all (thank God!) of exemplary life, suffer the same want, and have not bread to eat. A parish-priest, for instance, who lives a mile and a half from the town, is compelled to drag his own plough, to which he and some of his parishioners are yoked like horses. To conclude, sir, our Saviour is so good, that He seems to have specially granted to the people of St. Mihiel the spirit of devotion and of patience; for amid their extreme lack of temporal food, they are so anxious for spiritual sustenance, that we have not less than two thousand persons at catechism—a large number this for a small city in which most of the large houses are deserted. The poorest are very careful to be present, and to frequent the sacraments; and all classes alike have the greatest esteem for the missionary who is here, and who instructs and consoles them, considering it a happiness to have spoken to him even once. He is so engaged in works of charity and in the many duties of his office—indeed, he is so overwhelmed with general confessions, and so exhausted through want of proper food, that he has at length fallen sick."

We must not dwell longer upon so painful a theme. Suffice it to say, that Vincent employed his influence with Cardinal Richelieu, and obtained the removal of the French force from St. Mihiel, and thus in some measure relieved that place from the heavy pressure which weighed upon it; and by his abundant alms he did still more to save it from utter ruin.

The efforts of the missionaries were not limited to the towns we have mentioned; indeed, they may be truly said to have extended throughout the length and breadth of Lorraine; for wherever distress called for help, there was Vincent and his faithful band. And what point was there in that desolated land which needed not assistance? But the details we have given will more than suffice to illustrate alike the dreadful misery of the people and the exertions of our Saint for their relief.

It is scarcely possible to form an accurate estimate of the money expended in this charitable work. Abelly says, that Vincent collected and sent at different times nearly sixteen hundred thousand livres to the poor of Lorraine; and Collet (another excellent authority) proves, from documents which he examined, that it amounted to two millions of livres—a sum which, according to the value of money at that time, is above one hundred thousand pounds sterling!—alms worthy alike of a great city, of the occasion which called them forth, and of the Saint to whose energy and perseverance the good work owed its beginning and its completion. Few would have had the courage to take in hand a task so great, and still fewer would have succeeded in carrying it through. But Vincent's zeal was guided by profound wisdom; the resolution he formed was grounded on full consideration and a careful weighing of the whole matter; and thus, when difficulties arose, they never took him by surprise; he was prepared to meet and to overcome them in the strength of Him whose glory alone he sought. That the hand of God directed and blessed this undertaking, no Christian can for a moment doubt; but the special providence which watched over it showed itself in a manner which was little, if at all, short of miraculous.

In times of such disorder there was no protection for the traveller. Disbanded soldiers infested the country, who no longer assumed the flimsy pretext of military authority for their exactions, but conducted themselves openly as robbers; while utter ruin and inevitable starvation urged many a wretched creature to attempt the life of his fellow-man whenever he chanced to meet with one less destitute than himself. In consequence of this well-known condition of the country, no one who had any thing of value about him would venture to travel alone; nor was money ever sent from place to place without a strong escort. And yet, in the very worst of these unsettled times, Vincent sent a solitary unarmed brother of his order from Paris into Lorraine with large sums of money about his person; and this not once or twice only, but fifty-three times in the course of the nine or ten years during which the distress continued. From place to place this unprotected priest passed through the midst of misery and wild confusion; but never once did robber successfully assail him, never once did he lose even a fraction of the twenty or thirty thousand livres he carried with him.

It was not that Brother Matthew Renard, for that was his name, met with no adventures, or that he escaped without difficulty the many dangers which beset his way; few men had stranger tales to tell than he on his return to Paris from one of these expeditions. Indeed, he was so great a hero in his way, that the queen herself was fain to see him and listen to his narratives. It gives one quite an insight into the manners and habits of the age, to mark the quaint simplicity prevailing amid the formality of a royal court, which could allow of poor Brother Renard's being admitted into the august presence of Anne of Austria to tell his story. How must Vincent's eyes have beamed with more than their usual sweetness and good-nature, as he brought his shrewd messenger to the graceful and kind-hearted queen; and how must they both have smiled at the recital of the clever stratagems by which the justly-named Renard preserved their alms from the hands of the spoiler! Of a truth, he had many a tale to tell; and it is only fair that we should admit our readers to the conference, and let them listen while he relates to his royal patroness how, to use his own words, "the God of Vincent de Paul journeyed with him, and guarded him on his way."

Sometimes he joins a convoy which is attacked, but he is sure always himself to escape; now he parts company with his fellow-travellers to their loss, for they are plundered almost as soon as he has left them; on another occasion he perceives some robbers or disbanded soldiers in a wood, he throws his purse into a bush, and then advances boldly towards the marauders, displaying ostentatiously his empty wallet, like a man who has nothing to fear. Of course, they search him from top to toe, and equally of course, gain nothing for their trouble, and so let him pass. As soon as they are out of sight, back the poor brother goes to pick up his purse, and carries on in triumph perhaps a hundred thousand livres. Once he had a very narrow escape; for travelling with a large sum about his person, he was suddenly attacked by a horseman, who, not wishing to search him on the public road, made him walk before his horse with a pistol at his head towards a more retired spot. How could Renard conceal his money? He never despaired, but watching an opportunity when the robber chanced to turn his head, he threw his purse upon the ground. And now Brother Renard became vastly polite, and made various bowings and scrapings before his captor. The robber paid no attention to what he considered mere tricks to awaken his compassion, and drove him on before him, but not till Renard had made footmarks enough on the ploughed land which they were crossing to recognise the spot again. At last the robber stopped, and searched the missionary close to the edge of a precipice. We may imagine the fate which would have awaited the poor brother, had this large sum been found upon him, for "dead men tell no tales;" but as nothing was discovered, he was allowed to pass on, in due time to return to the scene of his manœuvre and recover his money.

Innumerable were the adventures he met with, and wonderful was the fertility of his wit in devising expedients for escaping from those who waylaid him. His oft-repeated journeys attracted attention, and it soon became known that the missionary was the bearer of large sums of money. His danger thus increased; ambushes were laid for him, which he generally escaped; or if he was taken, he was sure not to have a farthing about him. The conclusion was natural: the evil-disposed declared he was a sorcerer; the poor, whom he relieved, regarded him as their guardian-angel. Vincent applauded his skill, and the queen enjoyed and triumphed in his successes.

We have not quite finished yet with Lorraine and its troubles; for Vincent's work of charity is still incomplete. The father who had been sent, as we before mentioned, to visit the different parts of that province, reported on his return that a great number of young women, who had lost their parents in the wars, or during the subsequent distress, were in great poverty; and that they were exposed to the insolence and violence of the soldiery who occupied the country. Vincent consulted the ladies who had so often helped him in difficulties; and it was decided that the missionary should return to the duchy, and bring back with him to Paris all who wished to leave the scene of so much danger. But when he made his errand known, so large a number offered themselves, that he could only make a selection; and he returned accompanied by no less than a hundred and sixty of those whom he considered to be exposed to greatest peril. On their arrival at Paris, they were received by Madame Le Gras, who lodged them in her house. Here they were visited by the ladies of the association, who made their case known among their personal friends; and it was not long before these poor emigrants were provided with situations, either as companions or as servants, according to their condition.

But scarcely were these settled, ere another call was made upon the charity of Vincent, which he was the last person to withstand. The misery which he strove so nobly to relieve, drove multitudes from Lorraine to seek for help in other parts of France. Numbers of these poor outcasts came to Paris, and went straight to St. Lazarus, as though Vincent was their natural protector. His name was so intimately connected with the charity they had experienced in their own country, that by a sort of instinct they sought out the house of their benefactor. Thus was the quiet priory besieged with a host of applicants. None knocked at that gate in vain. If they were provided with letters of recommendation, they were, of course, admitted; and if not, their distress pleaded irresistibly in their behalf. For all these Vincent had to provide; and he placed them in the village of La Chapelle, about a mile and a half from Paris, where he gave them two missions in 1641 and 1642. Gladly did they avail themselves of these means of grace, of which the troubles at home had so long deprived them; and shortly afterwards they were employed either in domestic service, or in the trades which they had formerly followed.

Another class had yet to be assisted. Among the crowds which flocked from Lorraine to Paris were many persons of rank who had literally lost their all. Their position was far worse than that of their poor neighbours; for how could they make their wants known? or how could they endure to ask for charity, and lay bare their domestic sorrows before strangers? Fortunately some humane person discovered what they would fain conceal, and told the tale of woe to Vincent. Our Saint received the intelligence with a thrill of joy; for here was another grief to which he could minister. Far from shrinking from the additional charge which would thus be laid upon him, he exclaimed, with touching simplicity, "Oh, sir, you are doing me a great favour! Yes, it is but right to succour these poor nobles; it is a way of honouring our Saviour, who was Himself so nobly born, and yet withal so very poor."

The course which Vincent pursued was as delicate and considerate as charity itself could suggest. He called together some six or eight noblemen, and made them acquainted with the circumstances. As usual, his words imparted his own spirit to those who were brought in contact with him. They at once provided for the immediate relief of the sufferers, and deputed one of their number to distribute their alms, and to make such inquiries as should enable them to regulate for the future the amount of relief to be given, according to the necessities of each case. The young Baron de Renty was the person selected for this difficult task, and he discharged his office with all the zeal which might be expected in one who had so early in life given up a world which idolised him, to devote himself to the education of his children and to works of charity. He made his report, and the nobles subscribed among themselves enough for the requirements of a month; and so the good work went on from month to month for upwards of twenty years; and long after the original object had ceased, did it provide means for other needs, and thus became in Vincent's hands an instrument of continued usefulness. M. de Renty and his noble companions administered their relief with the same modesty and simplicity as had guided Vincent in first communicating to them his design. Their visits were those of friends and equals, not of patrons; there were no impertinent inquiries, nothing which could offend native delicacy, and that becoming reserve which grows more sensitive under suffering. No one's self-respect was wounded by the assistance which these nobles rendered to their less fortunate brethren.

When the wars came to an end, most of them returned to Lorraine, Vincent's thoughtful generosity providing for them even to the last. They received enough to carry them home, and to provide for them in their own country until such time as they could reconstruct their shattered fortunes.

place him in direct antagonism to Cardinal Mazarin; while his love of humility and of a lowly station must suffer severely by the dignity and grandeur of so elevated a position.

Vincent's penetrating eye had soon read the heart of Mazarin, and he saw how little there was in common between them. How, then, could he hope to carry out the pious intentions of the queen, when one so influential stood in his way? We shall see how he succeeded; but first let us take a glance at Cardinal Mazarin. As ambitious as his all-powerful predecessor, Mazarin pursued altogether a different course from Richelieu in aiming at the supreme authority. The one had gone straightforward towards the end to be attained, crushing whatever dared to oppose him; scorning to stoop to flattery or deceit, he awed all who came into his presence, and bent the most inflexible to his mighty will. Mazarin, on the contrary, was all suppleness and diplomacy; with bland smiles and ambiguous words he crept along, bribing where he could not cajole, and crouching where he could not otherwise win his way. If Richelieu was ferocious, it was with the heart of a lion; if Mazarin pleased, it was with the fascination of the serpent. If the former was an enemy, he was at least open and sincere; but the friendship of the latter could never be trusted. The man upon whom Richelieu frowned knew that he must stand aside or prepare for war; but few had skill to read Mazarin's countenance.

It was with Mazarin, such as we have described him, that Vincent had to contend; and though the contest may seem at first sight unequal, the plain-dealing and upright policy of the Saint were more than a match for the finesse and duplicity of the minister.

The particular duty which the regent assigned to Vincent de Paul was, to receive the petitions of those who sought for appointments, or who applied on behalf of others. He had to examine their claims and qualifications, and to report thereon. A more difficult or delicate task could scarcely be assigned to an ecclesiastic, or one more certain to expose him to misrepresentation and obloquy; yet, regardless alike of praise or blame, he cared only to do his duty to the regent and to the Church.

For a time Vincent met with little opposition from Mazarin, who was too busy in establishing himself in power to bestow much attention on the proceedings of his humble colleague; but before long the cardinal found him a sad impediment in the course of his policy. Mazarin had many enemies whom he desired to gain over: the great families looked with jealousy on this Roman adventurer, who had not long since been a soldier in the Italian campaign, and who had now, at Richelieu's advice, been placed in so high a station. They had feared the great cardinal; and now they hated and despised his legacy to the nation, the man of smiles and deceit. It was Mazarin's policy to buy those who stood in his way, and whose influence could thwart his purposes. Unfortunately he had precedent enough for regarding the emoluments and dignities of the Church as mere instruments of power and bribes to advance his ends. But this Council of Conscience came terribly in his way; and the upright, scrupulous, and fearless Vincent de Paul was the very worst person in the world to understand and sympathise with the difficulties and requirements of the minister.

It is alike amusing and instructive to watch the contest between the two. At first the cardinal pretended to ignore his colleague, and began to nominate, without consulting Vincent, to rich abbeys and to vacant bishoprics, looking only to his own interests and the influence he could thereby gain with this nobleman or with that great family. But Vincent quietly cancelled these appointments by refusing to approve them; and, as Madame de Motteville relates, the scheming minister found him to be a man *all of a piece,* who never cared to gain the good graces of the powerful men at court. The queen herself supported Vincent, and determined to allow the cardinal to make no such appointments without his sanction. Thus was his power confirmed, and Mazarin could only console himself by sneering at Vincent, and mocking the homely dress in which he appeared at court. "See," he exclaimed, taking hold of Vincent's old cincture, "see how M. Vincent dresses to come to court, and what a fine girdle he wears!"

Vincent could endure with a better grace the sneers of the cardinal than the respect and veneration which others showed him. The Prince de Condé one day tried his humility severely, when, meeting him at the Palace of the Louvre, he desired him to sit down beside him. "Your Highness does me too much honour in suffering me to remain in your presence," exclaimed Vincent, quite loud enough to be heard by the surrounding courtiers; "I who am the son of a poor swineherd." The answer of the prince was as graceful as it was true: "*Moribus et vitâ nobilitatur homo*—(Behaviour and a good life are man's true nobility). Besides," he added, to Vincent's great confusion, "it is not to-day that we have learned your merits."

That Vincent should offend many besides the cardinal by the firmness with which he resisted unworthy appointments, was only to be expected; but the extent to which people carried their anger, and the abusive language in which they indulged, could scarcely be credited in these days of refined manners and polished speech. On one occasion, a nobleman of very high rank failed in obtaining a piece of preferment for one who did not deserve it, and justly attributed his ill-success to the opposition of Vincent. Meeting our Saint a few days afterwards in the Louvre, he publicly insulted him in the grossest manner. The regent was informed of this behaviour, and commanded the offending nobleman to quit the palace. Vincent was overwhelmed with confusion at what would have been a triumph to any one else, and entreated that his reviler might be pardoned and called back; and so earnestly did he press his suit, that the queen was obliged to give way, in spite of the indignation she justly felt at the manner in which he had been treated.

On another occasion Vincent prevented the appointment of an improper person to a bishopric, and by so doing gave great offence to the family of the disappointed man. To revenge themselves, they invented a calumny against Vincent, to which they contrived to impart a plausible colouring. When the story reached the ears of the queen, she took the earliest opportunity of asking him if he had heard that such-and-such a thing was laid to his charge. "Madame," he replied, without any anxiety, "I am a sinner." "But," exclaimed Anne of Austria, "you must be defended." "They said many worse things against our Saviour," was Vincent's calm reply.

Once his equanimity was nearly overcome, when a report spread through Paris that he had bartered a benefice for a library and a large sum of money. Roused by this unjust attack, he took pen in hand to defend himself; but a moment's reflection caused him to throw it down, exclaiming: "Miserable creature that I am! what am I about? Do I wish to justify myself; when we have just heard that a Christian, falsely accused at Tunis, has endured torture for three days, and at last has died, without uttering a single complaint, although he was innocent of the crime laid to his charge? No, it shall not be." He rose from the table, and took no pains to contradict the calumny. When the propagator of the falsehood died shortly afterwards, not a few people saw in that death a token of divine judgment upon one who had tried thus to injure a faithful servant of the Lord.

In spite of the injunctions of the queen, who, as we have seen, forbade him to make any ecclesiastical appointments without first referring the matter to Vincent for examination, Cardinal Mazarin occasionally took advantage of our Saint's absence from court to nominate persons to whom he was under obligations, or from whom he expected support, to dignities for which they

L

were quite unfitted. Abelly has preserved an anecdote which shows how Vincent acted upon one of these occasions. One day he received a letter from the cardinal, who was with the court in the country, to the following effect:

"Sir,—These lines are to inform you that M. N—— has hastened down hither to ask for his son the bishopric of N——, which has been vacant some days. The queen has granted it to him the more willingly as he has the requisite qualifications; and, moreover, her majesty was well pleased to have so favourable an opportunity of acknowledging in the person of the son the services of the father, and the zeal he has shown for the welfare of the state. The queen has promised to write to you herself; but I have anticipated her, in order that you may take the trouble to see him, and give him such instructions and suggestions as you may judge necessary to enable him to discharge satisfactorily the duties of his office, &c."

The receipt of this note gave Vincent no small pain, and placed him in a very difficult position. On the one hand, he desired to pay all due deference to every act of the queen and of her prime-minister; but on the other, he well knew the unfitness of the person thus nominated for the episcopal office, and especially for the diocese in question, which was very extensive, and through a long course of neglect had been reduced to a most deplorable condition. What could he do? It was too late to apply to the queen or to the cardinal, for the royal warrant had already been issued; and even if he succeeded in cancelling the appointment, he might array against the crown an influence which at such a time was all-important. There was but one course open: remain silent he could not; and so he took a bold step. The family which had obtained this mark of the royal favour honoured Vincent with its friendship, and he at once betakes himself to the father who had thus unwittingly done his best to ruin the soul of his son. He arrives at their residence; and when the nobleman looks to receive congratulations upon his son's promotion, he hears from Vincent words which startle and perplex him. The Saint sets plainly before him the qualities and virtues which are necessary in a bishop, and contrasts with these the character of the young ecclesiastic. He then most solemnly warns him to return the appointment into the queen's hands, if he would not expose himself and his house to the wrath of Him who threatens with such severe punishments unworthy and mercenary pastors. The father trembles; he is not a bad or an irreligious man, but he has learned to judge with the world about sacred things, and to regard the emoluments and dignity of the position rather than the sacredness of the office and the heavy responsibilities it involves. He feels the truth of what Vincent presses with so much earnestness; and while he promises to consider his words, he has the grace to thank him for his unpalatable advice.

But, alas for the weakness of poor human nature! The good intention, which seemed for a time to influence him, vanished ere it could produce any fruit; the voice of conscience was drowned in the clamour of worldly considerations. In a few days Vincent had occasion to call upon this nobleman upon some other business, and he was received with the exclamation, "Oh, M. Vincent, you have disturbed my rest for several nights!" and then he had to listen to the usual excuses with which men strive to close their eyes to duties which are distasteful; the state of his affairs, his advanced years, the number of his children, and the duty of providing for them before his death. And then, to hear the means he had devised for surrounding his unworthy son with sage and holy councillors, and the good he expected the diocese would hence derive! The infatuated parent had persuaded himself that it was a positive duty to grasp at so glittering a prize. Vincent heard all in silence, and made no reply to reasons which could scarcely blind him who so warmly urged them. He had done his best to preserve a young friend from ruin; he could do no more: he left the matter in the hands of God. And terrible was the penalty which the family paid for the act of sacrilege. The new bishop, full of life and hope, had scarcely been consecrated when the hand of death smote him; and the broken-hearted father speedily followed to the grave the son whom he had sacrificed to his ambition.

One more anecdote we must relate, in connection with the trials which Vincent's firmness and uprightness brought upon him in the discharge of these delicate and arduous duties. A lady of high rank recommended her son to Vincent for a bishopric. As the Saint knew nothing of his character, he merely replied, that he would inquire into the matter; he did so, and finding the son to be unworthy of the appointment, he named some one else, who thereupon was promoted to the dignity. As soon as the lady was acquainted with the fact, she desired the servant of God to call upon her. Vincent went, accompanied, as usual, by one of the brothers, who waited in the ante-chamber, while he himself passed into the saloon. The lady received him with a torrent of abuse, and was so violent in her anger, that the brother, thinking her mad, rushed hastily into the apartment. As he entered, the fury hurled at the head of Vincent a heavy silver lamp, which struck him on the face. Vincent turned his bleeding countenance towards his affrighted companion, and said, as he quietly wiped away the blood, "It is nothing, my brother; it is only the excess of a mother's love."

Thus, amid many difficulties and much opposition, Vincent pursued the path which conscience had marked out for him in his high and responsible station. The good which resulted to the Church was great beyond expression. At any time so upright a minister could not fail to advance the cause of religion; but in such an age Vincent's appointment was an especial blessing. His indefatigable industry left no stone unturned which could bring to light any evidence respecting those who sought preferment, so there could be no excuse for the appointment of unworthy persons; while his diligence was equally great in finding out and advancing the interests of those whose modesty and worth shrank from that indecent contest for place which so generally prevailed.

The French Bishops found in Vincent a zealous champion and a faithful servant; while his prudence healed many a quarrel, which, but for him, might have had disastrous consequences. The practice of appealing to temporal courts, however well intentioned in its origin, had grown into a great abuse, and weakened considerably the discipline of the Church. Vincent's wisdom and charity corrected the evil in a way which could give a triumph to no party. He consulted with the President Molé to remedy the disorder, and at the same time humbly suggested to the princes of the Church, that mildness, patience, and even self-humiliation, ought to be their first weapons; and that they should never resort to excommunication until these had failed. His counsel was, that they should try before all things to reclaim those ecclesiastics whom the disorders of the times had corrupted; and that they should use the same means as our Lord had employed to convert sinners. It was his task, moreover, to bring back religious houses to the observance of their rule, and to infuse into them the spirit of their order. To this end, he prevented the appointment of superiors who owed their nomination to human considerations; and when the nomination lay with the king, he was sure to select the best fitted for the office, without any regard to political or personal interest. He was particularly anxious to prevent any thing like family interest or connection being mixed up with such appointments, and refused to sanction the recommendation of abbesses and others who wished their sisters or nieces to succeed them.

Vincent de Paul was a great church-restorer; and plenty of room was there for the exercise of this function in a land which had so long been ravaged by civil

and religious warfare. The zeal which in early life
had shown itself for the glory of the Lord's house in
the curé of Clichy, found full vent in the member of
the Council of Conscience. He was vigilant to see that
those who held livings kept their churches in repair,
instead of allowing them to fall into ruin, as was too
often the case in days when men scrupled not to receive
the incomes of parishes and abbeys which they never
deigned to visit. His authority procured edicts against
blasphemy and duelling, while it restrained the licentiousness both of the theatre and of the press. To him
is also due the credit of abolishing the evil custom of
rewarding military merit with ecclesiastical preferment;
but, at the same time, he was careful to secure pensions
for those who by their courage and services merited
well of their country.

It can scarcely be necessary to state, that Vincent
acted in a spirit of pure disinterestedness; that while
he sought out the deserving for promotion, and kept
back the unworthy, he had one object alone in view,
—the glory of God. Yet we may almost venture to
accuse him of injustice towards his own order, so careful
was he to avoid even the appearance of partiality. The
temporalities of the French Church may be said to have
passed through his hands; and yet no portion of them
reached his own houses. Poor, indeed, his brethren
were, and by their abundant alms they were frequently
reduced to absolute want; yet not only did he refuse to
solicit for them any share in that secular wealth which
he might so easily have obtained, but he absolutely
diverted into other channels the assistance which the
regent designed for them. We may here relate, that
it is stated on what seems good authority, that Vincent
had great difficulty in preventing the queen from procuring for him a cardinal's hat.

Such was the public life of Vincent de Paul. In
the midst of political intrigue, he busied himself alone
in the duties of his office. While others were striving
to advance their personal influence, or to aggrandise

themselves, his desire was to shrink back into the obscurity he loved, and to lay aside a dignity which had no charms for him. It was well for France that he was not allowed to abandon his post; for the power thus acquired enabled him to advance still more rapidly that moral and social reform to which his life was devoted. His missions benefited the lower classes; his exalted station brought his influence to bear upon the very highest. He had journeyed from place to place, and had thus made himself acquainted with the wants of the poor; he had seen how their spiritual welfare was neglected, how a vicious system of patronage had squandered among the undeserving the revenues which piety had dedicated to the service of God, and how the necessary results had too surely followed in the ignorance and barbarism of the people. He had toiled to alleviate the spiritual distress which the horrors of civil war had augmented; and now the time had come when he could attack these evils in their very source, and call in the aid of the highest civil and ecclesiastical power to root them out. It surely was a special providence of God which placed Vincent de Paul in the Council of Conscience, and gave him the power to carry into effect the reforms which he knew to be so needful.

CHAPTER XIX.

VINCENT AND JANSENISM.

These two names come together only as light and darkness, truth and falsehood, meet, to mark a contrast and illustrate a natural antagonism. The miserable heresy which bore the name of Jansenism raised its head in Vincent's path only to be trodden under foot by that faithful son of holy Church; but its propagator was brought into too close connection with our Saint for us to pass over altogether in silence the rise of what tended, for a while, to mar so considerably the great work which Vincent had in hand.

There were two students in the University of Louvain whom a similarity of taste and disposition had bound together in ties of closest intimacy. Cornelius Jansenius and John du Verger de Hauranne had alike imbibed the errors, which not long before had been condemned in the writings of one of the professors, Janson, and also in those of the Chancellor of the University, Baius. After leaving Louvain, they again met at Bayonne, the native place of Du Verger, where Jansenius remained for several years as a professor in the university; and there they devised a plan for re-establishing what they were pleased to call the doctrine of St. Augustine, which, they affirmed, had not been known in the Church for many ages. After a time they once more separated, and Du Verger became Abbot of St. Cyran in Berri. By this name he is best known in history, and with him we are principally concerned; for though Jansenius gave his name to the new heresy, St. Cyran it was who brought it into France, and by his energy and ability gave it a power which the book of Jansenius could never have imparted to it.

Of Jansenius little more need be said. He was made Bishop of Ypres in Flanders, and died, in the active discharge of his duties, of the plague, which raged with great violence in his diocese. He lived, however, long enough to complete his book, the *Augustinus*, which obtained such notoriety as the exponent of the new heresy, and from which the celebrated five propositions were drawn which were formally condemned at Rome. It is worthy of remark that, a few days before his death, Jansenius wrote to Pope Urban VIII. to declare, that if the Holy Father wished him to make any alteration in his work, he would submit himself to him with an entire obedience; and not many minutes before he expired he repeated this declaration, and added, with his own hand, that he had lived as an obedient son of the Church, and that he died in this obedience, and that such was his last wish. It is difficult, however, to reconcile with this seeming submission to the Holy See the fact, that Jansenius took every possible care to have his work published after his death without waiting for the Papal sanction. May not the crafty spirit of Jansenism be herein observed, even thus early?

But less ambiguous was the conduct of St. Cyran. In the year 1637, about a year before the death of Jansenius, he took up his residence in Paris, and there began covertly to introduce the heresy which had long fermented in his mind. Like most heresiarchs, he assumed a great austerity of life. He won the hearts of many by the zeal with which he declaimed in favour of the ancient penitential canons of discipline, and urged the necessity of reviving their observance. He deplored the coldness and ignorance of the age in which he lived, and thus drew around him those who aimed at a higher standard, and whose penetration was blinded by their sympathy with what seemed so holy and pure.

But St. Cyran had his eyes upon one whose influence was perhaps greater than that of any other man in the religious world of France. He ardently longed to gain Vincent de Paul and his community to his side, and to that end he sought and obtained the friendship of our Saint. Impressed with his zeal and energy, Vincent gladly met the advances of one who seemed to have the same object in view with himself, and many were the conferences which they had together. For a time Vincent remained in ignorance of the heretical opinions of his friend; but at last St. Cyran threw off the mask, and stood revealed before him in his true character. It was only gradually, however, that the truth broke upon our Saint. At one time St. Cyran astonished him by a defence of one of the errors of Calvin. Vincent replied, that the doctrine in question had been condemned by the Church; whereupon he received the astounding answer, *Bene sensit, sed male locutus est* (He meant well, but expressed himself ill); by which he intended to say, that Calvin's doctrine was true, but badly worded.

Abelly records some conversations between these two men, in which their characters and principles come out in strong contrast.

On one occasion St. Cyran had the boldness to maintain an opinion which the Council of Trent had condemned. "What, sir!" exclaimed Vincent, "do you wish me to believe a single fallible doctor like yourself rather than the whole Church, which is 'the pillar of truth'? She teaches me one thing, and you maintain the very opposite! Oh, sir, how can you venture to prefer your own judgment to that of the wisest heads in the world, and of so many prelates assembled at the Council of Trent, who have decided this point?" "Speak to me no more of that council," sharply replied St. Cyran, whose wounded vanity made him at the moment forget all discretion and prudence; "it was a council of Pope and schoolmen, brought together entirely by intrigue and faction."

The modesty and gentleness of Vincent's manner led St. Cyran to imagine that he could easily win him ⲧ to his opinions: he saw that, in spite of the strong language he had used, Vincent still occasionally visited him; and he interpreted this condescension into a disposition to yield to his opinions, when, in fact, it was occasioned solely by our Saint's anxiety to deliver his friend from the spiritual dangers with which he perceived him to be surrounded.

At length St. Cyran showed himself in his true colours. In a subsequent conversation he gave utterance to the following words, the folly and vanity of which are only exceeded by their blasphemy: "I confess to you," he said, "that God has given, and still gives, me great light; He has made known to me that there has been no Church for five or six hundred years. Before that time she was like a mighty river whose waters were clear and pure, but now what seems to us to be the Church is nothing but a slough. The bed of this noble river is still the same, but the waters are changed." Vincent replied with firmness, yet with his usual sweetness, "What, sir! will you rather believe your private opinions than the word of our Lord Jesus Christ, who said that He would build His Church upon a rock, and the gates of hell should not prevail against it? The Church is His spouse. He will never abandon it, and the Holy Ghost never ceases to assist it." Simple and conclusive as was this reasoning, it served only to increase the violence of St. Cyran. "It is true," he replied haughtily, "that Jesus Christ has built His Church upon a rock; but there is a time to build and a time to pull down. She was His spouse," he added, growing more and more heated, "but now she is an adulteress, a prostitute, and therefore it is that He has put her away; and it is His will that another should occupy her place." Vincent's countenance expressed the horror which he felt at such blasphemy; and St. Cyran, feeling that his hopes were gone, and that nothing could be gained from the devout missionary, turned with all the violence of his character upon one who had treated him with so much gentleness, and exclaimed passionately, "You understand none of these things; you are an utter ignoramus, and instead of being at the head of your Congregation, you deserve to be driven out of it altogether: I am only surprised that you are tolerated at all." "I am more surprised than you," was the quiet answer of the holy man; "I know well that if they did me justice they would not fail to send me away, for I am even more ignorant than you suppose me to be."

This was their last familiar interview. Vincent saw that he could do no good by arguing with one so lost in error and spiritual pride, and he could take no pleasure in the society of a man who indulged in such impiety. Before long Richelieu cast the heretic into prison at Vincennes. St. Cyran had made many friends, and these were now urgent with the cardinal for his release; but Richelieu was inflexible. He saw how dangerous the man was to the peace of the Church, and he had learnt wisdom from the mistakes of others. His reply was, that if Luther and Calvin had been treated in the same way when they first began to move, the Church and the world would both have been spared torrents of blood and of tears.

But quick as Richelieu had been to discern the true character and pernicious influence of St. Cyran, and promptly as he had acted upon that discovery, he was too late to accomplish the object he had in view. The seed had been sown, and the heretic had done his evil work, ere Vincennes had received him within its walls. He remained in prison four years, and was released only on the death of Richelieu in 1642. He lived but one year after; but long enough to see the heresy he had propagated inoculate with its poison many noble minds. Jansenius died, as we have seen, in 1638; and his famous work, the *Augustinus*, appeared in 1640. In this he teaches the heresy which bears his name, and which, among other things, denies free-will to man, makes God the author of evil, and rejects the doctrine of universal redemption. St. Cyran seconded with all his energies the posthumous work of his friend, and Port-Royal, where his influence with the Arnaulds was great, threw the weight of its mighty name into the same scale.

But a great blow was given to their combined efforts by Urban VIII., who in 1641 declared that this work revived the propositions of Baius, which had been already condemned by St. Pius V. and by Gregory XIII. The controversy raged with great fury in Paris for several years; Antoine Arnauld defending the new heresy in three successive "Apologies for Jansenius." It was at this time that Nicholas Cornet drew up the celebrated five propositions which embodied the principal doctrines of the *Augustinus*, and which were formally condemned by the Sorbonne in 1649. The Jansenists appealed to the parliament, and obtained an injunction that no further steps should be taken against them. It was then found necessary, in order to terminate the dispute, to urge the Holy Father to decide the question. This important letter to Innocent X. was drawn up by the Bishop of Vabres at St. Lazarus, under the eyes of Vincent de Paul, and signed by the Bishops who were present at the assembly of the clergy. It was then sent into the provinces to the rest of the episcopal body, and zealously did Vincent labour to induce all to unite in so momentous and necessary an act. Such was his success, that one alone, the Bishop of Luçon, refused to sign it; while two others suggested that the question might be settled by an injunction to both sides to refrain from controversy. To these remonstrants Vincent replied in a strain worthy of the occasion, insisting on the necessity of recognising the authority of the Holy See, and of submitting to its judgment. The petition went to Rome with the signatures of eighty-eight Bishops attached to it.

As might be supposed, the Jansenists did not remain idle during this movement. They failed in an attempt to dissuade the French Bishops from signing the petition, and then resolved upon sending three additional agents to Rome to assist one whom they had already commissioned to defend their cause in the ca-

pital of Christendom. The chief of these, Gorin de
Saint-Amour, was one of the most zealous of the faction, whose zeal, however, seems to have exceeded his
knowledge; for he afterwards declared that he had never
read the book which he was so ardent in upholding!
Vincent de Paul no sooner heard of this deputation
than he despatched three of his friends, who were doctors of the Sorbonne, to watch and counteract their
schemes; and difficult enough did they find their task
to be in overcoming the obstacles which the skilful
diplomatists cast in the way of an immediate decision.
But in spite of all opposition the cause progressed
rapidly. Innocent X. was then in his eighty-second
year; but with an energy unexampled at so advanced
an age, he carried through the examination of the five
propositions. Three times a-week was the venerable
Pontiff found in congregation with the cardinals, prolonging the sittings for three or four hours at a time;
and such was the influence of his example, that every
thing else was laid aside that this great question might
be fully and quickly determined. In 1653 the Pope
condemned the Jansenistic doctrines.

Great indeed was the joy of Vincent when the glad
tidings reached Paris; and at once he took all due means
to have the Papal rescript promulgated and obeyed.
The whole episcopate of France accepted it without
hesitation; not one even of the few who had been deceived by the Jansenists refused to pronounce the anathema. But, with a charity équal to his joy, Vincent
used every effort to unite together all whom this heresy
had separated; and to prevent the defenders of the good
cause from irritating by an appearance of triumph those
who had submitted to the judgment. He went to Port-
Royal, that stronghold of Jansenism, where St. Cyran
had been all-powerful, and where the family of Arnauld
all but worshipped his memory, and there, in the midst
of the chiefs and zealots of the party, he spent several
hours in kindly intercourse; congratulating them on
what was every where rumoured, that they had sub-

mitted unconditionally to the Papal decree. His heart was filled with joy, for all declared that the report was true; Peter had spoken, and therefore the matter was concluded.

But these fair promises were soon proved to be insincere; and no wonder, for deceit and equivocation are of the very essence of Jansenism. It had not even the hardihood of Protestantism, which openly abandoned the Church whose teaching it rejected; but it sought, by false dealing and ambiguous language, to retain a place within the one fold. Its policy was never outwardly to abandon communion with Rome; never, in so many words, to refuse submission to authority; but to resort to a host of subtleties for the purpose of explaining away the decisions of the Holy See, and in reality to persist in its rebellion all the time that it pretended to yield the most implicit obedience. Thus, on the present occasion, Arnauld took the lead in throwing doubts upon the condemnation. The pretence was, that the propositions condemned were not those of Jansenius; although, previous to their condemnation, they were allowed to be a fair exposition of his doctrines. To remove the doubts thus raised, thirty-nine Bishops assembled at Paris, in March 1654, and named a commission of eight of their body to examine the different interpretations by which the Jansenists sought to render the Papal rescript of no effect. Ten meetings were held, in which the text of the *Augustinus* was compared with the five propositions, and the writings put forth in defence of that book were most closely examined. The result was, that the committee declared, "that the Pope's constitution had condemned the five propositions as contained in the book of Jansenius, and in the sense of Jansenius." Innocent X. approved of this judgment in a brief which he addressed to the general assembly of the clergy of France in Sept. 1654; and in it he declared, "that by his former constitution he had condemned, in the five propositions, the doctrine of Cornelius Jansenius, contained in his book called *Augustinus*.

Equivocation could no longer avail the Jansenists in
this direction; so they turned their forces to another
point, and Arnauld put forth the opinion that the Church
is infallible only on questions of dogma, and not on dogmatic facts. Thus the controversy took a new form,
and raged as fiercely as ever.

When Innocent died, he was succeeded by Alexander VII., who had been one of the chief commissioners
in the examination of the five propositions. In 1656
he made a new constitution, by which he confirmed in
every point that of his predecessor. In this he described
as disturbers of the public peace and children of iniquity
those who maintain that the five propositions are not
found in the book of Jansenius; but that they are forge-
ries, and that they have not been condemned in the sense
of that author. This constitution was gladly received
by the general assembly of the clergy at Paris in 1657,
and by that body it was ordered to be published and
carried into execution in every diocese by the Bishops.
It also drew up a uniform formulary of faith, which was
to be every where subscribed. There seemed no loop-
hole for the cunning even of a Jansenist; but the skill of
the party devised a memorable expedient for escaping
from the authority of the Church and the formulary
which it prescribed. "No one," said Arnauld and his
party, "is obliged to submit *internally* to the judgment of the Pope on a question of fact. But the question on which the Pope has pronounced in the case of
the book *Augustinus*, is a question of fact. Therefore we are not obliged to receive, contrary to our own
light, what the Pope has pronounced in the case of the
book *Augustinus*." This famous syllogism subverts,
in effect, the authority of the Church, and indirectly
denies her right to judge authoritatively of dogmatic
truth or of error contained in books.

Pierre Nicole and Pascal employed their skill in defending this proposition, and turned away from the real
question at issue into an unimportant inquiry as to
whether the condemned propositions were contained in

Jansenius. It was never affirmed that those propositions were taken word for word from the book; but, as we have seen, competent authority had pronounced, after due investigation, that they were substantially contained in the *Augustinus*. The celebrated *Provincial Letters* of Pascal entirely evaded the real matter in dispute, and wasted their sparkling wit and graphic power upon a mere shadow, and in satirising those who had so damaged the cause he and his party had at heart. Even Voltaire confessed that Pascal built upon a false foundation.

In vain did Vincent use every effort to win back these self-deluded men to a loyal and true-hearted obedience. They persisted in their equivocation and deceit, and he directed his attention to the preservation of others from the poisonous errors which they were so industriously but stealthily disseminating on every side.

CHAPTER XX.

THE FOREIGN MISSIONS.

We have hitherto said nothing respecting the missions which Vincent de Paul and his community gave beyond the limits of France. To enter fully into this branch of the subject would require far more space than can here be afforded; we must therefore content ourselves with a passing glance, sufficient to show the beginnings of that great movement which in time carried the Lazarist Fathers into all parts of the world.

And first in the list must come the mission to Rome. In 1638 Vincent sent one of his Society to that city to arrange several important matters respecting the Congregation. This business was in due time despatched; but not before M. Louis de Breton (such was the name of the agent) had had the opportunity of carrying out in the neighbourhood of Rome the missionary schemes in which he had laboured so successfully at home. Indeed, his preaching met with such success, that Pope Urban VIII. expressed a wish that a house of the order should be established in the metropolis of Christendom. Four years elapsed before Vincent found the necessary means for accomplishing the wish of the Holy Father; but at the end of that time, thanks to the charity of the Duchess d'Aiguillon, a certain number of the Fathers took up their residence in Rome. The Pope at once engaged them in the arduous duties of preparing candidates for ordination by spiritual retreats, in visiting the hospitals, and in giving missions among the country-people.

There were peculiar difficulties in the way of these missions, which it required all the zeal and self-denial of the Fathers to overcome. The Campagna which surrounds Rome is, as every one knows, principally pasture-land, where herds of cattle graze, but on which no permanent residences are built, on account of the unhealthiness of the climate at certain seasons of the year. The malaria forbids more than a passing visit, and the consequence is that there are no villages; but the shepherds carry about with them wherewithal to construct temporary huts, which they erect wherever they may chance to pass the night. The question was, how to get hold of so nomadic a race, which, it was evident enough, could never be induced to frequent distant churches so long as they remained in their present ignorance and indifference. There was only one course to be pursued; if the shepherds would not come to the Fathers, the Fathers must go to the shepherds. For this purpose the missionaries wandered during the day over the Campagna; and having thus made acquaintance with the shepherds, and learnt where they would rest at sunset, had less difficulty in obtaining admission to their huts, and instructing them in their religious duties during the long evenings.

Suspicion and indifference could not long withstand the zeal and self-devotion of men who shared the simple fare and hard couch of these neglected people; and it was not long before many fervent penitents were kneeling at the feet of the missionaries, who with glad hearts prepared them for the Divine sacraments. When the different groups had thus in turn been visited and won, it was no hard task to bring them together in the nearest chapels; and there, on Sundays and holidays, might be seen feeding devoutly on the Bread of Life those who had long been looked upon as beyond the influence of Holy Church. A like success rewarded the labours of the missionaries in other parts of the Papal dominions, especially in the dioceses of Viterbo and Palestrina. Urban VIII. died in 1644; but his successors knew how to value as he had done the services of the Lazarist Fathers, and to their charge the retreats of the candidates for ordination were exclusively committed. It may serve to assist us in forming some idea of their labours in Rome to observe, that during the first twenty-two years of their residence in that city they gave upwards of two hundred missions.

Vincent, as the reader may remember, had been at Rome many years before, on his return from slavery. He had marked with a bleeding heart the neglected state of these poor shepherds; and now he is able to send them the aid he knew they so much required.

But while he bore in mind the neglected state of the shepherds of the Campagna, he felt still more irresistibly called to the succour of those poor souls who, in the states of Barbary, were languishing in slavery, and in hourly danger of apostasy. He had once shared their lot; and though he had tried hard to conceal from others the sufferings he had undergone, he had not forgotten them. The long-desired occasion at length presented itself. Louis XIII., in the last year of his life, gave Vincent a sum of five hundred pounds for this very purpose; and our Saint selected Julian Guérin for the arduous mission. Julian had not long joined the Congregation, and yearned with all the ardour of a novice for the crown of martyrdom. He had laid aside the profession of a soldier to place himself under the standard of the Cross; and his parting words were expressive of the true heroic spirit: "I only hope," he said, "that God will grant me the privilege of being impaled, or of suffering something worse, for His sake." His success at Tunis was wonderful. He gained the favour, not only of the Christians, but of the Mahometans themselves; even the Bey held him in high esteem, Christian priest though he was. And so, when he had toiled for two long years, and found that the work grew daily upon his hands, he told the Bey that he must have another priest to help him. The boldness of his request met with the success that so often rewards daring courage among infidels. The Bey listened with kindness, and granted his petition. He wrote home, and Vincent sent John le Vacher to be his colleague.

On his arrival at Tunis, Father le Vacher found a

pestilence raging with great violence; and soon fell under its baneful influence, from which he recovered only to lay his stricken colleague on a bed of sickness. From that couch Guérin never rose again. The martyr's crown was not granted him in the way he asked,—his was not a violent death; but surely the martyr's prize is as truly gained by one who faces pestilence in his Master's service, and who, like a true shepherd, lays down his life for the sheep. On Le Vacher the heavy burden now fell, not only of filling the place of him whom he had come to assist, but of occupying the responsible post of French consul, which had been left vacant by the death of one of the best friends of the mission. It was some time before Vincent could relieve him from this worldly care; but at last he met with one to whom, with the consent of the government, he could intrust so important an office; important in a worldly point of view, but still more in its relation to the Christian slaves, whom it was the consul's duty to protect.

Father le Vacher has recorded in his letters several instances of heroic virtue among the Christian slaves, amongst which the following has an especial interest for ourselves.

In the year 1648 there were two young slaves at Tunis whose pious conduct attracted much attention. They were about the same age, neither of them being more than fifteen; and having been purchased by masters who were close neighbours, the similarity of their condition naturally attached them to one another. One was an English Protestant, and the other a French Catholic; but it was not long before God's grace enabled the latter to bring the English lad to the true faith. Their sufferings were great; for their masters treated them cruelly, and their refusal to embrace the errors of Islamism embittered their owners still more against them. Their only consolation was in their common faith, and in the ardent affection which bound them together. It happened that, after a time, some English merchants came to Tunis for the purpose of liberating the slaves of their own nation. The English boy was on their list, and his freedom would have been secured, but that in abandoning Protestantism he had forfeited the sympathy of his fellow-countrymen. He plainly told them that he was now a Catholic, and that such he would remain; and so they left him in captivity.

The cruelty of the masters seemed every day to increase; the bastinado was applied to the feet of the two boys till they could feel no more; and often they sank insensible upon the ground, where their cruel torturers left them to recover their senses. One day the English boy found his friend nearly dead from the effects of the savage treatment he had received. Stooping over him, he called him by his name. What does he hear?—the poor lad regains sufficient consciousness to remember why he suffered, though not enough to recognise his fellow-sufferer, and he utters with a feeble voice the profession of faith which had so often brought the lash upon him: " I am a Christian, and I will remain a Christian." Overcome by the perseverance and the sufferings of the tender confessor, the young Saxon weeps affectionately over his friend, and reverently kisses the wounds of one who had done such great things for his soul. Some Mahometans pass by, and, observing the behaviour of the lad, ask him what he is doing. " I honour the limbs which have endured so much for Jesus Christ, my Saviour and my God!" and this heroic reply wins for him a renewal of suffering, and with the suffering an increase of merit.

When the French boy was sufficiently recovered, he paid his companion a visit; and found him in the midst of his tormentors, who were treating him with more than their usual cruelty. Exasperated at the sight, he cried, " Do you love Jesus Christ better than Mahomet?" The words rekindled the energies of the half-dead child; and gathering up what little strength remained, he exclaimed, " I love Jesus Christ above all things, and wish to live and die for Him." The anger of the infidels was at once diverted from their victim to the youth who had thus suddenly interposed; and one of them, who carried two knives in his girdle, advanced towards the lad, and threatened to cut off his ears. The spirited boy made a dash at one of the knives, seized it, and in a moment cut off one of his ears; then, holding it up to the infidel, he cried, "Do you want the other also?" Strange to say, from this moment the persecution ceased; the masters no longer tried to shake the constancy of these intrepid youths, whose faith seemed only to grow more firm by suffering. One more year, and their trials were at an end; the pestilence which then raged in the land bore them off to the reward which awaits such noble-hearted devotion.

But Vincent was not content with gaining an opening for his missionaries in Tunis; Algiers yet remained, with its 20,000 slaves, and in that place affairs were so badly managed by the French consul that there seemed a still greater need of succour. The first step was to obtain the recal of this inefficient officer, and to supply his place with a man of energy and true Christian spirit. Three missionaries were then sent, who speedily fell victims to the plague. Their places, however, were immediately supplied by others; and this mission, so costly in life and means, was carried on by Vincent's perseverance in spite of all obstacles and discouragements. During his life, it is calculated that upwards of 60,000*l.* were spent, in the states of Barbary alone, in delivering captives and satisfying the cupidity of their rulers and oppressors. The tender-hearted consul involved himself in heavy debts for the liberation of people who never thought of repaying him, and even Vincent had to exhort him to greater circumspection. But however costly these missions might be, the good they effected was beyond all price. The slaves, hitherto neglected and exposed to every danger of apostasy and moral ruin, were now carefully instructed in their duties and provided with the consolations of religion; the missionaries sought them out in their obscure prisons, converted the renegades, sustained the weak, and brought many an infidel into the true fold.

It was a fortunate day for Barbary when Vincent was carried into captivity; for the knowledge he then acquired led to the efforts we have just beheld for its spiritual gain. Men little imagined that the young student who, in 1605, was sold in the market-place as a slave, would one day send forth to the same spot those who should alleviate the miseries in which he then shared, and preach the faith which in his own person he had so well illustrated.

Another spot on which the zeal and devotion of the Fathers of the Mission found full occupation and met with complete success was Genoa. In 1645, the Cardinal Archbishop, Durazzo, called in the aid of the missionaries, and threw himself heart and soul into the work which was immediately begun. Genoa was in a terrible state; the people were plunged in the grossest ignorance, and preserved little more than the outward form of Christianity. The heart of the good cardinal was well-nigh broken, so unpromising was the prospect before him; but God upheld him in his untiring exertions for the poor sinners committed to his care, and in the end the reward was great. Ably seconding the efforts of the Archbishop, the missionaries brought to bear upon the diocese the whole of that spiritual machinery which had gradually been formed as experience suggested and occasion required; retreats in the city and large towns, spiritual exercises for candidates for ordination, missions in the rural districts, were carried on incessantly; and ever foremost in the good work was the cardinal archbishop himself, who became for the time as one of the missionaries, and conformed in every respect to their rule. Now he might be seen instructing the young ecclesiastics, now preaching to the townspeople, or addressing in simple and touching language the ignorant peasantry. The result was commensurate with the zeal and diligence of the labourers. The confessionals were not so much crowded as besieged, scandals were removed, and enmities of long continuance abandoned. At Chiavari, three parishes which had been at war for years were reconciled; at another place, family feuds were healed in which not less than twenty-four murders had been perpetrated. Indeed, such was the fervour of the people, that eighteen priests were continually engaged in the confessionals, and three thousand general confessions were heard, in which the penitents also required and received religious instruction.

The cardinal rejoiced in the success of the mission, and prized too highly the good which had resulted to let it pass away with those who had effected it. He determined upon founding a house of the order at Genoa, and three of his chief clergy nobly undertook the expense of the work. But not content with this, Cardinal Durazzo carried into the country-parts the different institutions which we have seen Vincent establish in France, especially the conferences, spiritual retreats, and associations of charity. So that, even among the poorest peasantry and in the most remote districts, Vincent's spirit animated and presided over the corporal works of mercy that were there performed; and where contributions were of the smallest, and the little annual subscriptions would almost excite a smile, the blessing of the Lord was on the widow's mite, and the cruise of oil failed not when poured forth without grudging for love of Him.

Such a mission was indeed after Vincent's own heart; and though his daily increasing infirmities forbade his being present in person with them, yet was his heart in the midst of their toils, while his fervent letters show how truly he made those toils his own. "O God"—thus he writes—"O my Saviour, be Thou the stay of their hearts. Bring into full bloom the flowers of those holy affections which Thou hast caused to bud within them. Increase the fruits of their labours, that the children of Thy Church may be sustained thereby. Rain Thy blessings upon this new house, as upon a nursling plant. Strengthen and console these poor missionaries in the weariness of their toils. And at the last, be Thou, my God, their recompense, and may their prayers obtain for me Thy infinite mercy." There were sorrows mingled with these joys which Vincent's tender heart felt acutely. A pestilence broke out at Genoa, which in 1654 raged so violently, that it carried off five or six of the chief missionaries; a loss, moreover, which was not confined to one diocese or kingdom, but in many places considerably reduced the numbers of the young order.

There is one more mission upon which we must dwell somewhat at length before we pass to the consideration of those which more intimately affect us. The next chapter will show what Vincent de Paul did for Ireland; we will conclude the present by recounting the first labours of the order among the heathen.

It was in 1648 that Innocent X., at the request of the Congregation for the Propagation of the Faith, sent a message by the nuncio at Paris to Vincent, desiring him to despatch some missionaries to Madagascar. That enormous island had been discovered by the Portuguese in 1506; but its terrible climate had soon driven them away, and at the time of which we write the French had possession of a fortified post which they called Fort Dauphin. A lofty chain of mountains runs through the length of the island from north to south, dividing it into two unequal portions. The interior is healthy and very beautiful; but the coast is throughout intersected with large lakes of stagnant water, caused by the closing of the mouths of the different rivers by high bars of sand which the ocean washes in upon the shore. The inhabitants of the coast are divided into two races, who respectively occupy the east and west sides, while the interior is held by a race quite distinct from the other two. The former is of African origin, not negro but hottentot; while the latter, the Hôvas, is evidently a conquering race of Malay descent, far superior in person and in intelligence to the dwellers on the seashore. It is not easy to obtain any very clear idea of the religion of these people; but they have a vague notion of a future life, and seem to have more fear of an evil spirit than love for a good one. Their chief sacrifices are offered to the former, who occupies the first rank in their religious ceremonies. They are in the habit of exposing the children who are born on Wednesdays and Fridays (their unlucky days) to the wild-beasts; but otherwise the Malagasses are sociable, kind, light-hearted, and fond of music and drinking. They have a plurality of wives, commonly as many as their circumstances enable them to support, though one alone is dignified with the name. The wonderful fertility of the alluvial soil renders labour altogether unnecessary; for rice dropped upon the ground, and pressed down with the foot, will yield a hundredfold. The timber is most luxuriant; but the undrained marshes of the coast, under the influence of heavy rains and the extreme heat at certain seasons of the year, exhale a malaria which no European constitution can long endure.

To this beautiful but pestilential island Vincent de Paul sent two of his missionaries in 1648. Their names were Charles Nacquart and Nicholas Gondrée; and at Vincent's direction they followed the example of the great missionary of India, St. Francis Xavier, and began their apostolic labours as soon as they went on board their vessel, which was at La Rochelle. It was on the Feast of the Ascension that they embarked; and Nacquart celebrated Mass on board the vessel and preached on the gospel of the day. His congregation consisted of a hundred and twenty-six persons, among whom were some soldiers and the new governor of Fort Dauphin. The very first thing we hear of as the fruit of this sermon was, that officers, soldiers, and sailors alike prepared themselves for a general confession, and those who needed it received catechetical instruction. After they had set sail, Mass was said daily, and spiritual conferences took place two or three times a week; all profane language ceased; in short, the vessel resembled a religious house. When they had nearly crossed the line, the wind became contrary, and the sailors talked of standing in for a harbour; but Nacquart, whose opinion was regarded as that of a sanit, advised them to proceed. He urged them to have recourse to Him whom the winds and the waves obey; and the company, binding themselves by vow to approach the sacraments at the coming festival of the Assumption, and to contribute towards a church to be erected at Madagascar under the invocation of "Mary, Star of the Sea," the wind changed, and all was well. They landed at Madagascar in December 1648, on which occasion Mass was celebrated, and a *Te Deum* sung in thanksgiving at Fort Dauphin, where for five months the Holy Sacrifice had not been offered.

Their first care was to begin the study of the native language; and while thus engaged, they employed themselves in the spiritual care of the French soldiers in garrison at Fort Dauphin. They found more obstacles here than they had encountered on board ship; for most of the men were living entirely without religion, and indulged themselves in plundering and ill-treating the natives. Father Nacquart began his intercourse with the Malagasses under very favourable circumstances; for he heard of a dian, or chief of a village, who had spent several years in his youth at Goa. At once it struck him that the man might have learnt something of Christianity while in that city, which was the seat of a Portuguese archbishopric. His conjecture was well-founded; the chief told him that he had been baptised, in token whereof he crossed himself and repeated the Creed, as well as the "Our Father" and "Hail Mary" in Portuguese. He readily gave the missionaries permission to instruct his people in Christianity, and himself assisted in the work. Before long other chiefs, who came to see what was going on, gave a like consent; and the two disciples of Vincent thus found a favourable opening, of which they were not slow to avail themselves. They redoubled their exertions in acquiring the language, and speedily learnt enough to make themselves understood. Thus prepared, they travelled from place to place; and made numerous disciples among the Africans, who were far more docile and anxious for instruction than the superior race—the Hôvas.

One night, as Father Nacquart was returning to Fort Dauphin, he passed through a village in which one of the principal personages besought his assistance. He was sick, and hoped that the missionary would cure him miraculously. The Father told him that God often sent bodily maladies for the good of the soul, and that perhaps He would cure him if he would cast aside his superstitions and embrace the true religion. "And what is this true religion?" asked the sick man. Nacquart gladly seized the opportunity of giving instruction; but with a prudent economy of his time and labour, he required that the inhabitants of the village should be called in, that they might hear what explanation he had to give. When all were assembled, he taught them plainly and with precision the principal articles of the Christian faith. The sick man listened with attention, felt consolation in the sublime truths, and declared that he believed all that the missionary had said. He desired to be baptised at once; but his teacher told him that a longer trial of his faith was needed before he could receive so great a blessing. Then, turning to those who were present, the good Father asked them what they thought of the Gospel; upon which they all expressed their pleasure at what they had heard. One of them, in his simple way, said that it was worth more than silver or gold; for these could be taken away by force, but the knowledge of God, when written on the heart, would always remain, and "one would always be sure to find it there on waking from sleep." The wife of the sick man had listened in silence to all that had passed; but now she spoke in a manner that both astonished and delighted the missionary. She assured him that for a long time past she had had recourse to

God; that when she sowed her rice or other grain, it was her custom to look up to the heavens and say, "It is Thou, O God, who canst cause the seed to grow which I plant, and who hast hitherto given me what I have reaped. If Thou hast need of it, I will give it Thee; and I wish to give a part of it to those who have none."

The missionary looked forward to receive before long the fruit of this unlooked-for faith, and to gather into the Church the harvest which had thriven so well. But an unforeseen event kept him away. His companion, Gondrée, was seized with a violent fever, brought on by over-exertion, and the neglect of some officers with whom he was obliged to travel; and Nacquart devoted to his sick friend every moment he could snatch from his flock and catechumens. In fourteen days Gondrée died, and with his parting breath sent his humble thanks to Vincent de Paul for the mission which he had given him. Nacquart was now alone: he felt that in time the terrible climate would lay him low, as it had done his dear companion; but he prayed to God to support him until others could come to carry on the work, and with a bold heart and untiring zeal he strove to fulfil the heavy duties which devolved upon him. To help the future missionaries, he prepared a translation of the Christian doctrine into the Malagassy language, which he committed to memory, and thereby acquired greater facility in speaking. But his journeys into the interior were now brought to an end. He could not leave the fort for more than six days at a time; for he was bound to say Mass there on Sundays and holidays. His ingenuity, however, contrived a plan by which he might still convey instruction to those whom he could not teach in person. He chose out the most devout of the French garrison, and prepared them as catechists; and then took advantage of every expedition into the country to instruct the natives as well by word as by example. The parts adjacent to Fort Dauphin he visited continually, instructing by day those whom he found in the villages, and at night those who were engaged during the day. In time his influence extended over the ruling class, who failed not to contrast his zeal and disinterestedness with the very different motives which influenced their own idolatrous priests. But anxious as the people showed themselves to be for baptism, he was very cautious in conferring it, reserving it for the dying, or for those who had given proof of perseverance; so that in eighteen months he did not baptise more than sixty.

It was in the year 1650 that Vincent de Paul received the letter which announced the death of Gondrée, and asked for some one to supply his place. Vincent mourned over the loss of so zealous a priest, and equally over the dangerous position of him who had alone to bear the burden and heat of the day. He determined upon sending more of the Fathers; but the war of the Fronde, which was now at its height, prevented for a time the needful succour. It was not until 1654 that the two priests whom Vincent had selected could set forth on their mission; and the next year he sent three more after them. It was a sad tale which one of the former had to send to our Saint, for it told how fiercely death had raged among them. When he and his companion arrived at Madagascar, they found Nacquart dead. His fellow-labourer lived but six months; and of the three last sent, one died on the voyage, a second soon after landing, and the third survived but a few weeks longer. Thus was the mission in the same state as when Nacquart wrote for help, and six missionaries had perished. But Bourdaise, the sole survivor, laboured with the utmost energy; and while he nearly overwhelmed the aged Vincent, who was now upwards of eighty, with the tale of woe, he comforted his heart with tidings of the great success which crowned the work which had yielded so many martyrs.

The loss of the missionaries, the reader will see, was contemporaneous with that which reduced so greatly the number at Genoa; while in Scotland more of the order were suffering severely. Thus sorrow seemed to accumulate upon Vincent; and could he have known that, while he was reading the sad letter of Bourdaise, that heroic priest was himself dying of fatigue at the age of twenty-seven, another pang would have rent his heart.

Many of Vincent's friends advised him to abandon the mission in Madagascar; but he felt it his duty to persevere. Difficulties continually interfered to prevent fresh missionaries from reaching the island. He sent two to join a vessel at Nantes: the vessel was lost before they reached it, and they returned to Paris. In 1658 he sent four more: the Spaniards captured the vessel, and the priests were sent home. Again, in 1659, he sent five of his Society to Nantes: the vessel had gone to La Rochelle; three of the number set out for that place by land, and two others went by water. The former sent word to Vincent that the latter had certainly perished with the vessel. It turned out, however, that this report was unfounded, and once more the party assembled at La Rochelle and set sail. But at the Cape of Good Hope the vessel went down; and though the lives of all were saved, the Fathers were forced to return. When they reached Paris, Vincent was dead.

In 1662, four priests at last succeeded in reaching Madagascar; and the mission continued with great success until Louis XIV. gave up the island in 1674, and forbade all French vessels to touch thereat. Four missionaries were at Madagascar at that time: the natives killed one of them, and burned a second in his house; the other two returned to France. One of these, Michael Monmasson, replaced Le Vacher in Barbary, and after saving many souls gained the crown of martyrdom.

CHAPTER XXI.

MISSIONS IN IRELAND.

IN May 1645 Rinuccini, Archbishop of Fermo, passed through Paris on his way to Ireland, to which country Innocent X. had sent him as nuncio. At that time Vincent was preparing, by the direction of the Holy Father, to send missions into Persia and the kingdom of Fez; but circumstances prevented the execution of these designs. It is very probable that the nuncio was the bearer of a message which directed the attention of our Saint to the deplorable condition of the land for which he was bound; for soon afterwards we find Vincent preparing no less than nine of his community for a mission to Ireland.

We must call to mind a few historical facts which will suffice to show the misery under which Ireland was labouring at that period.

During the unhappy disputes between Charles I. and his Parliament, the Irish Catholics remained faithful to the king. There was almost an infatuation in their attachment to that irresolute and faithless monarch; the many wrongs they suffered, they laid to the charge of his ministers; whatever gleam of sunshine penetrated the darkness that overhung the land, they attributed to the king. Even Strafford's government seemed mild, when compared with that of his successors; and the fall of that minister brought no consolation to those who saw in it but the triumph of their deadliest enemies.

Things had now arrived at such a state that they could no longer be endured. The rising of the Ulster chiefs in 1641 was a struggle for life; for the Puritans had vowed the extirpation of the Catholics; and before long the Catholics of the Pale were forced to join their more ardent brethren of the north. The country rose at the call, and the Church gave its sanction to what was felt to be a war of religion. A provincial synod of Ulster, held at Kells in March 1642, under the Archbishop of Armagh, declared the struggle to be a just and pious one; while a national synod at Kilkenny, in May, proclaimed the war to be lawful, "undertaken for the defence of the Catholic religion, and the preservation of the sovereign lord King Charles and his just rights and prerogatives." For a time success crowned the exertions of the confederates; but soon discord sprang up in the Irish camp. The "new Irish party," as the nuncio calls it in his report, the men of the Pale, began to tire of the league, and felt that they had little in common with the "old Irish." In spite of the earnest remonstrances of the wiser men, a truce was concluded in September 1643. It was a ruinous measure for the nation. A few weeks of active and resolute measures would have sufficed to annihilate the parliamentary party in Ireland; and who knows but that the forces, thus elated by victory, and attached so warmly to their king, might, by joining his friends in England, have brought the rebellion in that country to a very different issue from that which stained the nation with the blood of Charles I.? This unwise and hasty truce, however, ruined the cause.

In 1645 commissioners were appointed to conclude a peace, and at this time Rinuccini passed through Paris on his way as nuncio to Ireland. He arrived in October. Dissensions continued to prevail. The nuncio could not sanction a peace which gave no pledge for the free exercise of religion; but he was overruled, and the peace was formally ratified in July 1646. Rinuccini was not the man to sit down quietly under such circumstances. In August he went to Kilkenny with the great leader O'Neil, took the chiefs of the temporising party prisoners, excommunicated the authors and abettors of the peace, appointed a new council of eight laymen and four ecclesiastics, and was himself placed at their head as president. The people rallied round him; the king promised, if he could escape from the Scots, to throw himself into their hands; and the combined forces of Ulster and Leinster marched with their ecclesiastical leader after the lord-lieutenant Ormond to Dublin. However, the besiegers were obliged to retire without accomplishing their purpose; the curse of internal division, as usual, marred their councils; and Ormond, in opposition to the express command of the king, delivered Dublin into the hands of the Parliamentarians, and with the reward of his treachery withdrew to England, and subsequently to France.

Once more the confederates met with a reverse; several battles lost only fomented division. Another truce was proposed in May 1647, to which the nuncio again objected; it was carried, and once more he fulminated an excommunication. And now the controversy waxed still warmer, and divided the clergy, regular and secular, into violent parties. The Capuchins and Dominicans declared for the censures; the Jesuits, Carmelites, and Franciscans were for the truce; while eight of the bishops protested against the excommunication. Nor did the matter end here; O'Neil was proclaimed a rebel; and he replied by declaring war against the council. Before long Ormond returned to Ireland as lord-lieutenant; and the party which had before opposed him was now too much weakened by these divisions to stand in his way.

In January 1649 a new pacification was signed, and in a few days the murder of the king was perpetrated. The nuncio left the country; and in the same year Cromwell appeared on the shores of Ireland. In the month of August he landed at Dublin with eight thousand foot, four thousand horse, and twenty thousand pounds in money; for the regicides had sent him as lord-lieutenant, while Ormond retained that office in the name of Charles II.

It is not our purpose to dwell upon the awful scenes of rapine and bloodshed which marked the course of

Cromwell's army. One incident alone affects our narrative, and that brings us to Limerick. To that city had most of Vincent's missionaries betaken themselves, when, after a dangerous passage from Saint-Nazaire, at the mouth of the Loire, they reached Ireland. The holy company consisted in all of eight fathers, of whom five were of English or Irish birth; some went into the diocese of Cashel, but the rest, as we have said, repaired to Limerick. It was at the latter end of the year 1646 that they entered upon their missionary labours; and the result was such as to surprise the Fathers, though not greater than usually attends similar efforts among this devout people. The nuncio found time, amid the distractions of the civil war, to give his sanction to their work, and to recommend it as a model alike for bishops and priests; and these gladly availed themselves of its blessed influences. They were the first to present themselves to make a general confession; and by their example led on their flocks to a profitable use of the boon which Vincent had sent them. The disorders of the times had driven the country-people into the towns; and such were the crowds which beset the confessionals, that persons had to wait whole weeks before they could obtain admission. Those were, indeed, no ordinary times; the spirit of persecution raged with a violence which had scarcely been known before, even in that land of persecutions. And with that evil spirit rose the devotion of the people. The fury of the regicides turned with redoubled force upon the Catholics, who had dared to proclaim the son of their victim as king; and the missionaries found their occupation to be like that of those who, in the days of the early persecutions, prepared Christians for martyrdom. "As with the people, so with the priest;" not one of those among whom the missionaries laboured deserted his flock; violence or death alone could separate them.

But while their labours extended throughout the diocese, their chief exertions were directed to the city of Limerick itself, where was the stout-hearted bishop,

Edmond O'Dwyer. And well was it for Limerick that it had its bishop within its walls; for stout hearts were especially needed at that day, not only to bear up against the terrible sufferings which the faithful had continually to encounter, but to keep in the rugged path of duty those whose courage might be tempted to waver amid such severe trials. The good bishop was never missing, whether at the council-board or the altar; ready alike to give his voice for the defence of the city against the Independents and to minister at the death-bed of the plague-stricken famishing soldier. Ireton, Cromwell's stern son-in-law, was at the gates, and faint hearts trembled and talked of submission; nay, when the bishop threatened excommunication against the traitors, human weakness made some despise the spiritual penalty; but the negotiation failed, and the siege proceeded. Pestilence raged within the walls, and that so fatally, that not less than eight thousand of the inhabitants were swept away by this cruel malady. Many tried to escape from the city; but the brutal general threatened to shoot any who should attempt to come out. He actually seized three or four, whom he ordered for execution; and others he caused to be whipped back into the town. One of the poor creatures thus condemned to be hanged was a young girl, the daughter of an old man who was one of the number driven back. The father prayed to be allowed to die in the place of his child; but his prayer was rejected.

Thus the siege continued till the end of October 1651, when a traitor, Colonel Gennell, who had before betrayed the pass at Killaloe, and then taken shelter in Limerick, conspired with others, and treacherously admitted the enemy at one of the gates. The city being now invested on both sides by a numerous army, which had just received a reinforcement of 4000 men, the brave Hugh O'Neil and his garrison were constrained to accept articles of surrender. Ireton excluded by name from the benefit of pardon those who had been foremost in the defence; among these were O'Neil, the

Bishop of Limerick, and the Bishop of Emly. The first had a narrow escape. Ireton tried him by a court-martial, which condemned him to death; some of the officers remonstrated, and Ireton at length gave him a second trial, when he was saved by a single vote. The Bishop of Limerick escaped among the troops in the dress of a common soldier, and died at Brussels. For the Bishop of Emly a different fate was reserved.

Terence Albert O'Brien was a friar of the Dominican convent in Limerick, and was made Bishop of Emly in 1644. His eloquence was so powerful in sustaining the courage of the besieged, that Ireton actually made him an offer of 40,000*l.* and a passport, if he would only quit the city. He spurned the bribe, and was in consequence exempted from the pardon. He was tried, and condemned to be hanged and beheaded. In his last moments he addressed Ireton, upbraided him for his injustice, and summoned him to appear in a few days before the tribunal of God. The summons was obeyed! In eight days the inexorable general was smitten with the plague, and died raving wildly of him whose words he had so lately despised.

It was amid such scenes as these that the Fathers of the Mission toiled incessantly; and with what success we have already seen. It is, however, but just that the brave old bishop who bore so large a portion of the labour should tell his own tale, which he does in the following letter to Vincent:

"I have often in my letters to your reverence given you an account of your missionaries in this kingdom: to speak the truth, never, in the memory of man, was so great progress heard of in the Catholic religion as we have witnessed during the last few years, owing to their piety and assiduity. In the beginning of the present year we opened the mission in this city (where there are not less than 20,000 communicants), with such good success among the people generally, that I doubt not but that, by God's grace, the greater portion of them have been delivered from the grasp of Satan by the remedy which has been brought to bear upon invalid confessions, drunkennesses, swearings, adulteries, and other disorders which have been quite abolished; so much so, that the whole city has changed its aspect, being driven to resort to penance by the pestilence, famine, war, and other dangers which beset us on all sides, and which we receive as manifest signs of the anger of God. Nevertheless His goodness has been pleased to grant us this favour, unworthy servants as we are, to be engaged in this work, which, in truth, was so difficult in its commencement, that some even thought that we could never complete it; but God has made use of the weak things of the world to confound the strong. The chief people in the town are so assiduous in their attendance at sermons, catechism, and all the other exercises of the mission, that the cathedral can hardly hold them. We cannot better appease the anger of God than by extirpating sin, which is the foundation and cause of every evil. And, indeed, it is our own fault if God does not stretch out a helping hand to us. To Him it belongs to have mercy and to pardon. My father, I confess that I owe the salvation of my soul to your children. Write them some consoling words. I know not under heaven a mission more useful than this of Ireland; for were there a hundred missionaries, the work would always exceed the labourers. Our sins are very grievous; and who knows but that God may take from us His kingdom, and give the bread of angels to dogs, to our shame and confusion?"

Of the three missionaries who were in Limerick during the siege, one died in the discharge of his sacred duties, and the other two, Mr. O'Brien and Mr. Barry, escaped in disguise after the city had been taken. In 1652 they returned to France, after having laboured zealously in this country for six years. The whole expense of this prolonged mission was sustained by the funds of St. Lazarus; the only assistance which Vincent received being a present from the Duchess d'Aiguillon towards the expenses of the voyage, and for the purchase of some necessary altar-furniture. It is on record, that upwards of eighty thousand general confessions were heard; and, indeed, so wonderful were the results which followed, that it was proposed to Vincent to preserve some detailed narrative of the mission. His reply was striking:

"It is enough that God knows what has been done; the humility of our Lord requires of our little Congregation of the Mission that it should lie concealed with Jesus Christ in honour of His hidden life. The blood of the martyrs of Ireland will not be forgotten by Him, and sooner or later it will be fruitful in the production of new Catholics."

Surely it was in the spirit of prophecy that these words were uttered; and Ireland's subsequent history has borne noble testimony to their fulfilment.

But while the Fathers of the Mission were thus toiling in Ireland, Vincent was busy at home, assisting the people of the same land who had fled to France from the persecution which was raging in their native country. Cromwell was carrying his threat of extermination into execution, and numbers entered the French army to gain a subsistence. Many of these perished in the wars in Guyenne, and others in Picardy. The survivors, and the widows and orphans of the slain, were left in the extremity of distress. They had Troyes assigned for their winter-quarters; and a mournful sight it was to watch the poor sufferers as they entered the city, barefoot amid the snows of winter, and sinking under a nine days' fast; and people shuddered, as well they might, to see them devour with ravenous appetite what the dogs had left in the streets. As soon as the sad tale reached the ears of Vincent, he sent an Irish Father from his house with six hundred livres; and quickly there followed more money, as well as food and clothing. Thus the relief began; and the good ladies of Troyes soon followed the example which Vincent and his friends at Paris had set. The Irish priests had work enough to do in the spiritual care of those who could speak no language but their own; but the spirit of his order enabled him to prepare them for their Easter communion.

It is marvellous to think what our Saint was thus enabled to accomplish in the midst of the distress under which France was suffering at this time. The neighbourhood of Paris was uncultivated, and almost without inhabitant; the city itself was swarming with starving multitudes; and yet these poor exiles of Erin were tended with all a father's care!

CHAPTER XXII.

VINCENT'S TOUR OF VISITATION AND SUCCOUR OF PICARDY.

NEITHER our space nor our subject allows us to enter into the details of the war of the Fronde, that strange and disastrous event, which brought such suffering upon Paris and its neighbourhood, and threw for a time the whole nation into anarchy and confusion. But we may take a glance at the part which Vincent de Paul played in that extraordinary drama.

The violence of the parliament, seconded by the tumults of the Parisians, drove the queen and her council from Paris to St. Germain. She left the capital secretly on the morning of the 6th of January 1649. Vincent saw the danger which threatened the nation in the impending civil war; and while he disapproved of the violence of the princes and of the parliament, he regretted exceedingly the severity of the queen, who rejected all offers of accommodation, and issued commands to her general, the Prince de Condé, to blockade the city and reduce it to submission. In the excitement of such times Vincent well knew that he could take no step which would not at once draw down upon him the enmity of one of the two political parties into which the country was divided; but he felt that he was bound at any hazard to endeavour to put an end to such an unhappy state of affairs. His resolution was taken; he would see the queen and Cardinal Mazarin, and try to bring about a reconciliation. Accordingly, on the 13th of January, just a week after the queen's departure, the venerable old man mounted his pony, and leaving Paris long before daybreak, set out with a single companion on his arduous journey to St. Germain-en-Laye.

Dangerous times were those for travellers; for Paris was under arms, troops were quartered in the streets,

and patrols paced the faubourgs. Suspicion reigned in
every breast, and no man knew whom he could trust;
the sword was in each man's hand, and few cared to
inquire how and when it was used. Vincent and his
fellow-traveller had to make many a turn before they
could leave the city; but, thanks to the darkness, they
succeeded in reaching Clichy before broad daylight.
Here an amusing incident occurred, which nevertheless
serves to show the dangerous spirit which was abroad.
The people of Clichy had been plundered on the pre-
ceding day by a party of German mercenaries, and
were under arms expecting a second attack. In the
early morning they hear the sound of approaching
horsemen, and rush forth to meet their assailants; when,
to their astonishment, they encounter their old pastor
and his single attendant! More than six-and-thirty
years had passed since Vincent had ministered among
them; but the love his zealous services had kindled
glowed as warmly as ever, and the joyful tidings fly
from mouth to mouth that Vincent de Paul has come
again among his children. It needed not the contrast
which the apprehended attack of foreign foes afforded
to secure him a welcome; but the surprise gave a still
greater zest to their joy, and they overwhelm him with
proffers of service in every way, and carefully guide
him into paths where there would be less danger of his
falling into the hands of the enemy. After crossing a
dangerous bridge over the Seine at Neuilly, he reached
St. Germain about ten o'clock, and was immediately
admitted to an audience with the queen.

His remonstrance, though couched in respectful language, was energetic and firm. He pointed out how
unjust it would be to cause the death of such numbers
by starvation to punish the fault of a few, and he painted
in most striking colours the misery and demoralisation
which must be the result of a civil war. He plainly
told the regent that the presence of Mazarin caused
these disturbances, and that peace could not be restored
without the departure of that minister from court, at

least for a time. From the queen he went straight to
the cardinal, and repeated the same advice. With great
earnestness he begged the wily minister to "yield to the
storm, and rather to throw himself into the waves than
wreck the vessel of the state." Mazarin was little accustomed to such language; but he was touched, or at
least affected to be so, by Vincent's earnestness, and
quietly replied, "Very well, my dear father, so be it;
I will go, if M. le Tellier is of your opinion." Perhaps
the cardinal already knew Le Tellier's opinion; for when
a council was called the same day by the queen, the
secretary strongly opposed the design, and Mazarin
remained at the head of affairs.

Vincent had undertaken his journey solely for the
benefit of the people; yet it excited public indignation.
He was called a Mazarinist; and those who a week
before had revered him as a saint, now coupled his
name with every insulting epithet. Not venturing,
therefore, to return to Paris, he asked for a passport;
and the young king, to show his love for him, insisted
upon signing it himself, and gave him an escort as far
as Villepreux.

Our Saint was beyond the reach of his enemies;
but his house and community at Paris were at their
mercy; and quickly did those who, for their unworthiness, had been kept by him out of offices of trust,
vent their spite upon what the Saint held so dear.
The priory of St. Lazarus was seized by a party of citizens, headed by a magistrate, who pretended to act
with the authority of the parliament. They set guards
at the gates, and quartered within its walls a hundred
soldiers, and more than eight hundred of the cowardly
rabble who had just before fled in dismay from the
troops of Condé, and who reserved their valour for an
attack upon the inoffensive members of a religious
house. They plundered the Fathers of all that the
place contained, and then set fire to the outhouses.
The parliament was ashamed of its friends, and ordered
them to quit St. Lazarus; but no compensation was

ever made for the injury done. The principal support of the Fathers was derived from a large farm in the neighbourhood of Versailles; but marauding parties had made such havoc, that it supplied neither cattle nor corn. Vincent received accounts of all these reverses with his usual equanimity. "Blessed be God!" "God's will be done!" were his favourite exclamations; only he was careful to write back word that the poor should not be deprived of their usual relief, however dear corn and other food might be.

When Vincent quitted St. Germain, he betook himself to a farmhouse belonging to his order at Villepreux, near Etampes, where he intended to remain during the troubles, which he hoped would soon be ended. And here the aged and toil-worn Saint gave himself up to exercises of penance and of rigid mortification. In the severity of winter he but rarely kindled a fire, and then only of a few dry brambles; while his scanty food was limited to dry bread made of beans and rye. But while thus occupied in the care of his own soul, he was as diligent as ever in ministering to the wants of those about him. He preached repeatedly to the neighbouring poor, exhorting them to bear patiently the heavy trials of distress and famine to which they were exposed; and his words bore fruit in the salvation of many souls. The winter advanced; but the civil war came not to an end. Vincent, therefore, determined upon extending his visit to the houses of his congregation. The season was unusually inclement; a wet autumn had broken up the roads and inundated the country; and then a continued frost had turned into sheets of ice the whole of these stagnant waters. Few ventured out of doors; but nothing could stay the zeal and energy of the lion-hearted old man. Pressed down with years, and tortured with severe bodily infirmities, he once more mounted his pony, and reached Mans in the midst of a violent storm.

The astonishment of the brethren may be conceived at the unexpected arrival of their father at such a season; it was only equalled by their joy. After spending many more days than he had intended at this house, where the chief persons in the neighbourhood overwhelmed him with attentions, Vincent directed his steps towards Angers, in which city the Sisters of Charity had one of their principal houses. On the road, he nearly lost his life in crossing a river which had been greatly swollen by the rain and snow. The priest who accompanied him succeeded in rescuing him; and he went on his way as though nothing had happened, and in the evening reached a small roadside inn. It was Lent, and Vincent had tasted nothing that day. The old man, upwards of seventy-three, was shivering with cold in the wet clothes in which he had fallen into the river; and his first care is—what does the reader suppose?—to catechise the servants of the inn. Truly his food was to do the will of Him that sent him! The hostess, alike surprised and edified by this act of charity, ministered to his wants in the way which she saw would please him most; she sent out for the children of the village, and led them into his presence. Vincent thanked her cordially; and, separating the boys from the girls, he gave one class to his companion, and himself taught the other. With untiring energy he continued to instruct his simple auditors; then bestowing some alms upon them, he dismissed them, and at last thought of supper.

From Angers Vincent continued his journey to Rennes. On his road he a second time narrowly escaped a fatal accident on an insecure bridge; but God preserved him. One night he arrived at a forlorn cabin, where he was put into a wretched chamber, though it was the best the place afforded; but some friends of the peasant coming in, he had to exchange it for a filthy garret. On leaving the next day, he gave his host more than was his custom. A few days afterwards he arrived late in the evening, worn out with fatigue, at a village inn. Scarcely had he lain down, when a crowd of rustics entered an adjoining chamber, and spent the night in drinking, shouting, and rioting. When he went away in the morning, so far from complaining of the disturbance, he presented his host with some beautiful *Agnus Dei's* which he had intended for the Duchess d'Aiguillon; so thankful was he to all who gave him an opportunity of exercising patience.

Without delaying longer upon the incidents of this journey, we may remark, that from Rennes Vincent went to Saint-Méen, where he arrived on Maundy Thursday. During the fifteen days that he remained with the brethren in this house, he gave the community his rules, and busied himself with all the energy of a young man in the duties of the mission—preaching, hearing confessions, and catechising. He had visited Nantes and Luçon, and was about to proceed on his visitation to Saintes and to the other houses in Guyenne, when an order from the queen-regent recalled him to Paris. In obedience to the royal command, Vincent turned his pony towards Paris; but the severe labours he had undergone in the late inclement winter were too much for his exhausted frame. With great difficulty he managed to reach Richelieu; and there fell sick, and could proceed no further. As soon as intelligence of his illness reached Paris, the infirmarian of St. Lazarus came to nurse him; and Vincent knew not whether to rejoice at the presence of one he loved, or to grieve at the trouble his sickness had caused his friend.

The Duchess d'Aiguillon sent a carriage to fetch him to Paris. There is a story connected with this same carriage which is too characteristic to be passed over. It has been mentioned in a previous chapter, that Vincent had in former years changed places with a convict in the galleys, and that the chain which he wore had inflicted permanent injury upon his ancles. From time to time he suffered severely in his legs; but in his old age he altogether lost the use of them, and could not walk at all. He purchased a horse; but so old and infirm was the animal, that he not unfrequently endangered Vincent's neck by his stumbles and falls. One of his friends gave him three hundred livres to buy a better steed; but while he delayed the purchase a case of charity came before him which required just that sum, and what more natural than for Vincent to give away his money, and content himself with his old horse? Some of the ladies of the Confraternity of Charity now took the matter in hand, and had a kind of carriage built which was so simple and unpretending in its appearance, that they hoped even Vincent would not refuse to accept it; but the idea of a carriage of any kind quite shocked the humble man, and though he did not reject it, he suffered it to remain unused in the stables of St. Lazarus.

Now it was this carriage which the Duchess d'Aiguillon brought out of its retirement, and sent with a pair of horses to bring Vincent from Richelieu. The Saint could not but use it; for the commands of the queen were urgent, and he was unable to mount his horse. But no sooner did he reach Paris than he sent back carriage and horses to the duchess, with many expressions of gratitude. Once more they appeared at St. Lazarus, with an earnest request that he would use them, in consideration of his great age and many infirmities. Vincent again refused them, and declared that if the swelling of his legs prevented him from walking and riding, he would stay at home the remainder of his days. The duchess was as persevering as the Saint; she inherited Richelieu's spirit as well as his wealth, and having recourse to the queen and to the Archbishop of Paris, she obtained a positive order for Vincent to accept the carriage and horses, and to use them whenever he had need. Poor Vincent was overwhelmed with confusion at appearing in what he considered to be a style far above his position; and he called them his shame and his disgrace. One day, going to see the Fathers of the Oratory, he said to those who accompanied him to the door, "See, my fathers, see how the son of a poor peasant has the audacity to drive through the streets in a carriage!"

Vincent's equipage was now often to be observed in the streets; and much amused were the public to see the companions of his drives. Any poor creature going to a hospital, or sinking by the road-side, was sure to find a seat therein; and many were the stories which the good people of Paris told in connection with Vincent and his carriage.

Vincent had been recalled to Paris on the occasion of the return of the regent and the young king, in August 1649; but before long the peace which had led to this return was broken; Condé, Conti, and others, were sent to Vincennes by Mazarin, and the second act of the drama of the Fronde began, which is known by the appellation of the War of the Princes. The contest lasted till the year 1659; but we are here only concerned with the misery it caused, and the part which Vincent took in its relief.

The Spaniards, in league with the rebels, devastated Picardy and Champagne, and quickly reduced those flourishing provinces to a state similar to that in which we before saw unfortunate Lorraine. In 1650 Marshal du Plessis-Praslin forced the Archduke Leopold to raise the siege of Guise. Paris was in a tumult of joy at the good news, and paid but little attention to the reports which daily reached it of the misery of the people in the late theatre of war. Not so Vincent de Paul. The old man, in the midst of his infirmities, is as active as ever in a work of charity; and with the help of some friends he sends off two of his missionaries with five hundred livres and a horse-load of provisions for the sick and wounded. The ministers of mercy could not reach the scene of misery before their store was exhausted by those who were starving on the roadside. They hastened to the nearest town to purchase more food, but encountered the same destitution, which every where prevailed. Whither could Vincent turn for help? The war of the Fronde had reduced Paris

and its environs to extreme distress; his own resources
were well-nigh exhausted; while the ladies of his association were nearly overwhelmed by the claims of the
orphans and hospitals, and the ten years' succour given
to Lorraine. The Archbishop of Paris agreed to make
a general appeal to the city; and Vincent drew up a
short and touching statement of the misery which called
for relief. The call was nobly responded to; sixteen
missionaries and some Sisters of Charity were quickly
sent into Picardy, with a large supply of money and
provisions.

There is no need to describe the terrible sufferings
which these missionaries alleviated; scenes as horrible
as those in Lorraine daily met their eyes; and for nearly
ten years did this state of things continue. We may
form some idea of the amount expended, from the fact,
that during the earlier years of the distress it varied
from seven to fifteen hundred pounds a month. And
while these large sums were being sent to a distance,
the Fathers and others were equally busy in assisting
the population in the immediate neighbourhood of
Paris, who were suffering but little less severely. The
house of St. Lazarus was nearly empty; all except a
few old men, who were too feeble to take part in the
work save by their prayers, were labouring in this extensive field of charity. Even Paris itself was in a
most deplorable condition. The blockade, the destruction of the harvest by hostile armies, the stoppage of
all works and manufactures, the influx of strangers from
the devastated provinces,—all combined to make the
capital rival in misery the poorest and most desolate
of the provinces. Here again was work for Vincent
and his friends: fifteen thousand poor to be fed daily;
dwellings to be provided for religious who had fled from
ruined monasteries; nine hundred young maidens from
convents to be protected and supported. And in the midst
of all these trials, a new affliction visited the devoted city
—the Seine overflowed its banks, and spread destruction
no all sides. Vincent's resources were all expended;

but when he knew not where else to turn, he was sure to find a friend in Anne of Austria. The charity of the regent knew no bounds; when her money was gone, she gave her jewels. One day she sent Vincent a diamond worth 350*l.*; and on another she took her earrings from her ears, and sent them to the ladies' association, where they were sold for nine hundred pounds. It was the wish of the good queen to conceal these acts of charity; but Vincent made them known, that others might imitate her right royal example.

Thus on all sides is there distress and misery enough to weigh down the energy and charity of any man. But Vincent bravely bears up against it all; his stout heart faints not, his exertions never slacken; he seems to grow young again, that he may respond to every call, and with superhuman zeal achieves whatever he undertakes.

But though the demands of charity are answered, the frame of the old man sinks in the effort. There is a limit beyond which human nature cannot go, and the over-wrought body yields at last to the attacks of inveterate disease. The apostle of charity becomes at last the martyr of charity.

CHAPTER XXIII.

THE HOSPITAL OF THE NAME OF JESUS, AND THE GENERAL HOSPITAL.

ONE might have supposed that the day for Vincent to establish new institutions had passed, and that when he had reached his eightieth year he might have rested at least from the labours and anxieties of such undertakings. But it was not so to be. Two years before, he had gone on several missions, he had founded a seminary for Scotch children, who in due season were to be sent as priests to their own country to continue the work which the Fathers of the Mission had begun; and now his last great public benefaction grows up under his hands, and completes the cycle of those noble institutions with which his name is connected.

One day a citizen of Paris came and placed in his hands a large sum of money, to be employed as Vincent should think fit. One condition alone was attached to the gift, that under no circumstances should the name of the donor be revealed. Our Saint prayed that God would make known to him the special use for which He designed this offering; and after gravely and maturely weighing the matter, he went to lay his plan before the generous merchant.

It seems to have been the especial mission of Vincent de Paul to alleviate suffering. From first to last he took it under his particular care, and extended towards it a hand of succour at every stage of life and in every variety of form. In earliest infancy his foundling asylum rescued its victims from death, and brought them within the one fold of Holy Church; training them in holy ways, and educating them to fill useful offices in society. His Sisters of Charity sought out and instructed the poor and neglected, watched beside the bed of suffering when friends grew weary, and poverty made itself most heavily felt; his Ladies of Charity tended the sick in hospitals, and ministered to the occasional wants of such as could generally support themselves; while every diseased or afflicted spirit might find consolation and direction in the missions and retreats which the Fathers of St. Lazarus so constantly gave. Indeed, it was difficult to find a want which had not its remedy already provided by the zeal and devotion of the apostle of charity; and Vincent therefore might well pause before he determined in what new way to employ the noble offering which had been placed at his disposal.

But at last he devised a scheme, which he laid before the good citizen of Paris, and which met with his most cordial approval. He determined to found a hospital for aged artisans, wherein they might finish their lives in the exercises of religion, freed from those anxieties which poverty renders so harassing in old age. Vincent immediately set to work to carry into effect this new design, and bought two houses and a large open space in the Faubourg Saint-Laurent. He fitted up an excellent chapel, and thoroughly furnished both houses. What money remained he invested for an annual income, and at once received twenty men into one house, and twenty women into the other. Of course, the two communities were entirely distinct; yet the chapel and the two refectories were so arranged, that both could assist at Mass and hear the spiritual reading at meals without seeing one another.

Their time was so ordered, that they had sufficient occupation, in spiritual exercises and light labours, to employ their minds and their hands without distressing their decaying powers. The Sisters of Charity assisted them; and the priests of the Mission supplied them with all needful instructions, saying Mass for them and administering the sacraments. Vincent himself was frequently among them, giving advice and devising little rules which sanctified all their actions, and converted the establishment into a kind of religious house. He bestowed upon it the title of the Hospital of the Name of Jesus. The archbishop gave his sanction, and the king his letters-patent to the institution; yet so jealously did Vincent preserve the secret of its founder's name, that neither king nor prelate knew to whom to ascribe the work of charity.

A house so well regulated naturally attracted the attention of those who were best fitted to profit by its wholesome discipline; and Vincent was too prudent and vigilant to allow any but such as could be thus characterised to enter under its roof. It long continued a model hospital, a refuge for the aged, where the assistance which charity provided was administered in the spirit of love, and received with heartfelt gratitude. Here were no trustees to divert the funds to their own profit; no officers to swallow up the greater part in salaries and perquisites; and therefore no discontented pensioners to quarrel over the miserable pittance which maladministration doles out.

Like most of his institutions, this hospital led the way to other similar foundations. There is a fecundity about Vincent's acts which is quite marvellous. Every seed he sows brings forth a hundredfold. Like a stone cast into the waters, every work he performs is the centre of a motion which extends itself in ever-expanding circles; but with this great difference, that its power increases with each expansion, and the widest and most distant motion is frequently the strongest and the most influential. So was it with the present work of charity; it led to another of far wider scope, which dealt with a greater evil than Vincent and his unknown friend had ever hoped to overcome. Among the visitors whom the new hospital attracted to its walls were the ladies of the association of which we have so frequently spoken; and natural enough was it that they should contrast the piety and happiness of Vincent's pensioners with the misery and dissoluteness of the poor who swarmed in Paris. Need we say that they did not content themselves with instituting this very obvious contrast? The reader by this time will have learnt to distinguish these excellent women from those who think they have done their part when they have lamented over what they take no pains to remedy; and turn away with sensitive repugnance from the sufferings of the poor, simply because they are unpleasant to look upon. And yet if any amount of rudeness and vice could justify neglect and apathy, the beggars of Paris would have afforded that justification; for we have terrible descriptions of their blasphemy and debauchery. The fierce tones in which they demanded rather than solicited alms, the threats of violence with which in open day they extorted relief, and which at night they frequently enforced by robbery and murder, would naturally excite any feeling rather than that of compassion; but a deep and all-embracing charity impelled these generous souls to devise some application of Vincent's scheme to these miserable outcasts of society.

It was a bold imagination which suggested the founding a hospital for all the poor of Paris. There were at that time upwards of forty thousand mendicants in the city and its suburbs; and what kind of mendicants we have just seen. It was indeed a gigantic undertaking; yet they felt that success would crown their efforts if only they could induce Vincent to assist them. Such confidence had they, that they began at once to collect funds among themselves, and succeeded even beyond their hopes; one lady giving 50,000 livres (2500*l.*), and another an annual subscription of 3000 livres (150*l.*). Elated by this success, they called a meeting of their association, and laid their scheme before our Saint. Vincent was astonished; accustomed as he was to great efforts and wide-spread charity, he was staggered by the vastness of this undertaking; but he did not condemn it. He praised them for their generous design, but required time to consider before God what should be done. A week passes, and another meeting is held. The ladies return with increased zeal to the work; they see their way towards raising the necessary funds, and insist on making a beginning. Vincent himself allows that the thing is feasible, but recommends more consideration, and tries hard to moderate the impetuosity of the ladies. In vain; the question is put, "Shall the association undertake the responsibility of such a hospital or not?" and every voice replies in the affirmative.

Vincent hesitates no longer. He applies to the king for a grant of the Salpêtrière, which was a large building well suited for the purpose; and Anne of Austria, as usual, assists him in the application. No time is wasted in fitting up the building thus granted with all that was required; and some of the ladies are so anxious to commence operations, that they absolutely wish not only to receive at once all the poor who are willing to enter, but to force every beggar in Paris into its walls. "We wish to benefit them," they said; "and what does it matter how we bring them to our institution?" In short, they would have seized upon every mendicant who fell in their way, and compelled him to accept the blessings they had provided.

Vincent had now better grounds of opposition; and their good sense soon yielded to his quiet reasoning, when he showed them that large works of charity, like those of nature, must grow gradually, and from small beginnings, if they are to be permanent. "The desire to do every thing at once," he said, "is a temptation, which, like all other temptations, must be resisted. Our Lord might, had He so pleased, have established the Church in His own time in every part of the world; but He was content to lay the foundation, and to leave the rest to His Apostles and their successors. We must not think that all is lost, if every one is not anxious to co-operate in our plans. What we need is, to go on quietly, to act in harmony, and, above all, to pray earnestly." He then proposed that they should make a trial with one or two hundred who would come of their own accord. If they succeeded with these, others would speedily offer themselves; and thus the institution would grow by degrees into its full dimensions, and no fear need be entertained but that it was of God.

But there were others who threw serious obstacles in the way of the hospital, even in this modified form, and who forced Vincent to delay the work longer than he wished. It required the sanction of the magistracy; consequently the letters-patent of the king had to be registered by the parliament; and here a powerful opposition arose. Many members thought the scheme rash and extravagant, and declared that the public safety would be endangered by collecting so large and disorderly a body in one place. Vincent had much trouble in overcoming this obstacle; but patience, and the influence of his friends, at length carried the day. Yet, after all, so many practical difficulties presented themselves, that two years had passed before the institution could be settled upon a firm basis. In April 1656 the king issued an edict, vesting the administration of the general hospital in a body of twenty-six gentlemen of experience and approved probity.

It was rather in accordance with the original idea of the ladies than with that of Vincent, that it was determined that every beggar in Paris should be compelled either to earn his own living or to enter the general hospital. Vincent transferred to the authorities the house of Salpêtrière, and also that of Bicêtre, which the queen-regent had before granted him for the foundlings; and it was announced from every pulpit in Paris, that on the 7th of March 1657 the general hospital would be opened, and that after the said day no one would be allowed to beg in the streets. It surprised nobody to find that on the appointed day the great majority of the idle beggars disappeared as by magic; yet four or five thousand remained, of whom the greater part thankfully availed themselves of the great institution provided for them; and those who had laboured so zealously in its foundation had cause to rejoice in its success.

Vincent declined the appointment of spiritual director alike for himself and for his order, but recommended as rector of the hospital one whom he knew well, and in whom he had the greatest confidence. This was Louis Abelly, at that time a parish priest in Paris, under whose management a spirit of order and discipline grew up in the house which bore abundant fruit in the sanctification of its inmates. After a time Abelly was promoted to the bishopric of Rodez; but at the end of three years he resigned that dignity, and came back to Paris to finish his days in the Priory of St. Lazarus. To him we are indebted for the earliest and best life of Vincent de Paul; and from his abundant materials most of the subsequent biographies of our Saint have been drawn.

CHAPTER XXIV.

DEATH AND CANONISATION OF VINCENT DE PAUL.

The sufferings with which Vincent was afflicted increased from day to day; yet his attention to the many duties which pressed upon him continued unabated. And many and various indeed were they; for there was scarcely a work of mercy undertaken in France without his being consulted; and many a stranger came from other countries to lay his plans before the great apostle of charity. Letters poured in upon him from all sides, which he made it his business to read attentively and to answer fully. Responsibilities appeared to multiply with his increasing years; and others seemed as little to consider the burden they were laying upon the aged man as he did himself.

For some years past he had been unable to walk; but now his infirmities prevented him from moving down stairs, so that he was obliged to say Mass in the chapel of the infirmary. After a while he entirely lost the use of his limbs, and could no longer stand at the altar. His only consolation was in assisting at Mass, and in communicating every morning; daily might the aged servant of God be seen dragging his powerless limbs into the chapel by the help of crutches. In vain his friends besought him to allow an altar to be fitted up near his chamber, that he might hear Mass without undergoing so much fatigue; he refused the indulgence, and with difficulty consented to be carried to the chapel in his chair. He could not endure the idea of giving trouble, or of doing any thing unusual. His nights were as full of suffering as his days, and every little comfort which might have alleviated his pains was most resolutely rejected; for he would take nothing more than the rule directed, and would omit no practice which that rule enjoined. Thus he still continued to rise at four, and spent three hours in prayer before Mass. He felt that he was gradually sinking; but as throughout life, so at its close, he was quite indifferent whether to live or die, whether to suffer pain or to obtain relief. His only prayer was that the will of God might be done.

Those who visited him at this time found him as patient, as cheerful, and as tender-hearted as of old. He was as busy as ever in works of charity, as careful to give each one about him the necessary directions, and as willing to listen to all who could plead any or no excuse for troubling him. Who that heard that voice so blithe, whose tones had all the music of charity; who that beheld those eyes beaming with the fervour of devotion, or watched that sweet angelic smile, which bespoke the innocence of his soul, would have guessed the continual agony which racked his exhausted frame, as he sat there in his chair, clad in his usual dress, so calm and gentle, and spoke of his sickness so lightly and unconcernedly? Yes, there he sat, awaiting the call of his Lord and Master, and daily renewing his preparation. Every morning after Mass he repeated the prayers of the Church for those who are in their last agony, and the commendation of a departing soul; while every night he made ready to meet the Judge whom he had served so long and faithfully. Deep humility, that surest test of sanctity, dwelt in his heart, and spoke from his lips in lowliest accents of self-condemnation. "One of these days," said he to those about him, "the miserable body of this old sinner will be laid in the ground; it will turn to dust, and you will tread it under foot. Alas! my Lord, I live too long; for there is no amendment in me, and my sins multiply with the number of my years."

And now the news spreads through Europe that Vincent de Paul is dying; and the universal Church is moved at the coming loss. The Sovereign Pontiff, Alexander VII., writes and begs him to husband his strength, and dispenses him from saying office; and many of the chief ecclesiastics in Rome urge him to accept the dispensation. But when these letters reach Paris Vincent is dead: his breviary was never laid aside; his office was said up to his last hour.

Some days before his death he became subject to frequent attacks of lethargic heaviness, which he recognised as sure forerunners of the last great sleep. "This is the brother," he said with a sweet smile; "the sister will not long delay her coming;" and then he prayed those who stood around him "to excuse the trouble he gave them." On the 25th of September this lethargic sleep came upon him at noon, and lasted longer than it had ever done before. The following day was Sunday, and Vincent was able to hear Mass and to communicate; but scarcely had he been carried back to his room before he fell into a heavy slumber. The brother who was attending upon him roused him several times; but he quickly relapsed. The physician was sent for, who acknowledged that nothing more could be done, and that Extreme Unction might be administered. He then roused him once more, and spoke to him. Vincent answered him calmly, but after a few words he stopped; his tongue refused its office, and he had not strength to finish the sentence.

His spiritual children now saw that they were on the point of losing him, and collected around their father; and one of the priests of the mission begged him to bless them. Vincent with difficulty raised his head; he had heard the request, and would grant it, cost him what pain it might. With a look of deepest affection he raised his hand, and, with a strength of voice which astonished them all, he began the formula of benediction; but soon his voice sank, and the concluding words could scarcely be heard.

The same night he received Extreme Unction, and occupied himself in contemplation and in communion with God. Occasionally he fell into a doze; but the single word "Jesus" sufficed to arouse him. When that verse of the sixty-ninth psalm met his ear, "O Lord, make speed to save me," he tried hard to reply, "O God, make haste to help me."

At a quarter-past four, on the morning of the 27th, M. le Prêtre, who was a member of the Tuesday conferences, and one of Vincent's particular friends, being at that time in retreat in the house, came into the chamber. Vincent was in his chair, from which he had not moved for twenty-four hours because of his extreme weakness. M. le Prêtre begged him to give his blessing for the last time to the company to which he belonged, and to pray God that it might never degenerate from its first fervour. The dying saint, instead of a blessing, gave a promise, replying in the words of St. Paul, "He who hath begun a good work in you will bring—" his voice failed him ere he could complete the verse, and he bowed his head and expired. The lamp had burnt itself out, the oil was exhausted; and thus, without an effort, calmly and peaceably his spirit returned to Him who gave it.

No change passed over that benign countenance. Vincent seemed sleeping in his chair; but he was with God. The trials of life had passed,—its duties had been fulfilled; and, like him whose words were the last upon his dying lips, he had finished his course, he had kept the faith, and he had gone to receive the crown which was laid up for him in heaven.

The Fathers of the Mission were saying matins when Vincent de Paul died, on the 27th of September 1660, in the eighty-fifth year of his age.

The body, which remained perfectly flexible, was exposed, first in the house, and then in the Church of St. Lazarus, until the following day, when it was enclosed in a leaden coffin. The heart of the Saint, however, was deposited in a silver vase, which the Duchess d'Aiguillon presented for that purpose. All Paris followed him in crowds to the grave; high and low alike strove to testify their love and reverence to one who had been the friend and benefactor of every class. His body was interred in the centre of the choir, and on his tomb is inscribed the following epitaph:—" *Hic jacet venerabilis vir Vincentius à Paulo, presbyter, fundator seu institutor et primus superior generalis Congregationis Missionis necnon Puellarum Charitatis. Obiit die 27 Septembris anni 1660, ætatis vero suæ 85.*" (" Here lies that venerable man, Vincent de Paul, priest, founder or institutor and first general superior of the Congregation of the Mission, as also of the Sisters of Charity. He died on the 27th of September 1660, in the eighty-fifth year of his age.")

All felt that they had lost a dear and generous friend. It was not as if they knew him only by report, or that he had occasionally crossed their path; he was something far more than a mere prominent character whose virtue was extolled and zeal commended by those who knew him only by hearsay; Vincent had been among them, sympathising with every sorrow, and relieving every distress. When their souls were oppressed with sin, into his ear the tale of misery had been poured, and from his lips the words of ghostly counsel and comfort had flowed. Did they yearn, amid the false glitter and fierce struggle of the world, for something higher and purer than they had before known, Vincent was there to point the way, and to cheer them on by his bright example in the narrow path. The tones of his voice, his very smile, were familiar to most of them; and few indeed who had seen and heard but had learned to love and venerate.

It was a sad day for thousands when the grave closed over him; and many a bitter tear they shed, not for his loss, but for their own. For who should now guide the Fathers of the Mission? who should watch over the many charities which he had founded? who should care for his orphans, for his Sisters of Charity, for his poor prisoners? who should minister to the wants of whole provinces, and sustain the Church of France at the high standard to which he had raised it? Grief might thus question; but faith would quickly reply, The spirit of Vincent de Paul remains; it has not passed away with his life on earth. And experience has long since proved what faith would have suggested. The work indeed was Vincent's. The impress of his mind is stamped upon it; and through time it must bear those sweet tokens of its earthly father. But in another and a higher sense it is the work of God. Vincent was but the appointed instrument for its accomplishment; the Church trained him for his labour of love; she gave him the means by which he wrought it; through her he fulfilled his part; and when he went to his reward, she carried on the work she had herself inspired. And therefore, while we love and venerate him who spent himself so entirely and ungrudgingly in the service of God and of his brethren, our devotion is the more inflamed towards her who is the pure Spouse of Christ, and the fruitful Mother of Saints. As of Christianity itself, it may with all reverence be said of what Vincent wrought, that if it were of man, it would have come to nought, but being of God, it will abide. It has stood the test of two hundred years; and not one leaf of Vincent's wreath of charity has fallen. Storms of civil strife, such as the world never saw before, have passed over the land which Vincent blessed; every human institution fell before them; yet his work abides. And how abides? not as a curious relic of past times, which poetry embalms and taste admires; not as an institution which is upheld by force of law, and barely maintains a sterile and languishing existence; but with all the freshness of perennial youth, with all the vigour of robust maturity, it flourishes in its native soil, and continually sends forth branches into every quarter of the world.

Vincent had been dead thirty-seven years before his spiritual children moved for his beatification. They had learnt from their founder not to be hasty in any important matter. In 1697 the examination commenced of several miracles which had been wrought at his tomb. The jealous scrutiny with which the Church so wisely examines the testimony adduced in such cases prolonged the inquiry for several years; but so convincing was the result, that Clement XI. was overwhelmed with letters in favour of the beatification of Vincent. To show how wide the feeling extended, and how many great personages participated in the general desire, it will suffice to mention the King of France, the exiled James II. of England and his queen, the Grand Duke of Tuscany, the Duke of Lorraine, the heads of the Genoese Republic, besides a crowd of Cardinals and Bishops, among whom are conspicuous the names of Bossuet, Fénélon, and Fléchier.

One day the commissioners were carrying on their inquiries at Marseilles, and chanced to ask an old blind convict if he had known Vincent: "Oh, yes," he replied, "I made my general confession to him; he was a very holy man. But why do you ask me about him?" "They are going to canonise him," was the reply. "You are wasting your time," cried out the old man; "M. Vincent will never allow that; he was much too humble to suffer any such thing." Could there be higher testimony to the profound humility of the Saint?

In 1705 the assembly of the clergy of France petitioned the Sovereign Pontiff, and the process began. It was difficult among so many authenticated miracles to make a selection, and at first sixty-four were chosen; but to shorten the inquiry, a smaller number was at last named to be submitted to that rigid examination, the most severe which human evidence ever undergoes. Among the miracles thus tested and proved were the following cases of *instantaneous* and *complete cures* wrought at Vincent's tomb.

A young man who had been blind for eighteen months recovered his sight. A young girl who had been dumb and paralysed in all her limbs from her birth received the use of her tongue and limbs. Mathurine

Guérin, Superior of the Sisters of Charity at Paris, was cured of an ulcer in the leg, with which she had been afflicted for three years, and which had been pronounced incurable by medical treatment. Another case was that of a young man completely paralysed in his feet and hands, who was brought to the tomb, and walked away with the complete use of his limbs.

Vincent de Paul was beatified by Benedict XIII. in the year 1729. New miracles followed upon the declaration, and in 1737 the bull of his canonisation was published by Clement XII., and the servant of God was proclaimed a SAINT, with the usual solemnities, in the church of St. John Lateran.

Sancte Vincenti à Paulo, ora pro nobis.

Our task is done. There are many incidents in the life of St. Vincent which have not been noticed; many works of which we have not spoken; for what space would suffice to record the details of so long a life, and one so crowded with good works? But enough, we trust, has been told to show what Divine grace enabled one poor man to do for the glory of God and the benefit of his fellow-creatures. Without the advantages of birth or fortune,—for he was but the son of a poor peasant in an obscure village,—without those mighty gifts of intellect which oftentimes supply the lack of worldly influence,—in times of great spiritual desolation and national distress, Vincent de Paul conferred greater benefits on his country and on mankind than any one of those whose names stand highest in his nation's roll of fame. With no profound speculations and no elaborate schemes, he alleviated public distress, and raised the ecclesiastical character from a state of degradation to a position of honour and respect. With no rhetorical skill, he stirred the heart, not of a class, but of a nation. Himself no politician, he swayed in many important matters the mind of a Richelieu and of a Mazarin.

What, then, was the secret of his success? It was this: he had one idea, one aim. There is a wonderful power in the devotion of one unselfish will to a life-enduring object. No temptation can lure it from its path, no opposition can discourage, no adversity can daunt, no suffering can crush. Amidst the changeful moods, varying interests, and short-lived passions of all around, it pursues its way with its eye fixed on the goal of that race which is not to the swift nor to the strong, but to the persevering. If such be the case even in human affairs, how much more may it with truth be said of those whom God has raised up from time to time to accomplish some great work in the Church! The heroes and conquerors of Christian annals have been emphatically men of one idea and one aim; and Vincent de Paul differed not from his brethren in exalted sanctity. He placed himself entirely and unreservedly in the hands of God, having no other desire but to please Him and to do His will. He gave himself up body and soul to do his Master's work with an undivided heart and an inflexible purpose. He beheld his Saviour in every one with whom he had to do, and honoured Him in them. In the illustrious house in which he spent so many years, he tells us that he never entered the presence of his patrons without seeing God's greatness in them. No poor sufferer did he relieve but he worshipped in him the "Man of Sorrows." Did he grow faint under the heavy burdens which charity imposed upon him, there was refreshment in the thought of Him who rested in weariness by Jacob's well. Was he consumed by the fever which scarcely ever left him, or tortured by the terrible ulcers which for years made every movement excruciating suffering, he sustained himself by the memory of the Agony in the Garden and of the Passion of the Cross. Therefore it was that he could smile on all, and that he was cheerful in the darkest hour. But more than all, the secret of his success was this, that He whom he so loved was ever with him, or rather in him; working with his hands, speaking by his lips, and imparting power and virtue to his blessing. We need not marvel, then, at his success; he had faith, and therefore he wrought wonders.

But if the greatness of the work he achieved, by the aid of human means apparently so inadequate, be matter of surprise to the many, to the thoughtful, perhaps, it may seem more wonderful that one who was involved in such multifarious employments, and forced into so much intercourse with the world, should still be able to maintain such close union with God, and to preserve a spirit of such perfect recollection. It was the severe discipline by which he ruled his life, which upheld him amid the distractions of his laborious career. They who saw Vincent only in the business of daily charity, hastening through the streets of Paris on some errand of mercy, or to attend some committee of his many institutions, with beaming countenance and kind word for all, little thought, perhaps, of the early rising, the long meditation, the office recited on his knees, the daily Sacrifice, the hours of silence, and the scant coarse fare. The unction of prayer was upon him, and its fragrant graces flowed over upon all who came within his influence. No wonder that men grew better in his presence, that children clung fondly to him, that sin-hardened hearts grew tender, and that the sick recovered, as he drew near. He came like Moses from the Mount; and the glory of the Divine Presence was, as it were, visible round about him.

Such a man could venture forth safely into a world which he visited only as an apostle of charity. His actions, his works, flowed not from a spirit of busy active benevolence; they were the outpourings of that love of which he had drunk deep at the foot of his crucifix: Calvary was ever before his eyes; Calvary was set up in his heart. His rule was a simple one; and in that rule he found at once both safety and success: he first gave himself wholly to God, and then to the work which God set him to do.

To estimate aright the work which Vincent de Paul accomplished, we must compare the France of his early days with the nation as he left it when he went to his reward. He found the clergy degraded, and religion itself neglected. The name of *priest* was a title of contempt; and those who held rich abbeys and high ecclesiastical preferment, generally as the reward of military or political services, took every opportunity of convincing the world that they were not of the despised order. It was his privilege to raise up into due honour that rank which ignorance and neglect had thus degraded; to exclude the unworthy from positions of importance; and to train the young for the due discharge of their sacred duties. He saw and deplored the state of the clergy; and he devoted his mighty energies to raise and reform it. We have seen him founding seminaries for the young, and colleges for the more advanced students; instituting spiritual retreats for those about to be ordained, and conferences to sustain the true ecclesiastical spirit among the clergy; and guiding the councils of kings and queens in the selection of persons for the highest stations in the Church.

And while the clergy, from the lowest to the highest, were profiting by his zeal, we have beheld him busied among the laity of every rank, fitting them for their share in the national advance. He found the poor plunged in ignorance and sin, uncared for by those who should have been their guides in spiritual matters, and left to perish of hunger by their temporal lords. He instituted his Order of the Mission to relieve the wants of their souls; and by his untiring energy he raised and distributed enormous sums of money among starving provinces. He called to his aid, on the one hand, the clergy, whom he trained and elevated, and on the other the laity of every class, in whom his fervent charity kindled a like spirit. We have seen him, not so much quickening the zeal of those with whom he came in contact, as breathing into a cold and heartless generation a spirit which was indeed of God. We have watched his influence spreading on every side, until all ranks of life vie with each other in following his guide

ance, and in pouring into his treasury the riches of
their charity. War, famine, and pestilence combined
to ravage whole provinces; and Vincent brings relief to
each and all. To what quarter can we turn and not
meet him? What want is there which he does not discover and minister unto? For the sick in hospitals he
devises his confraternities; for those who need nursing
at home he has his Sisters of Charity; for foundlings
he has his asylum; for the poor who need temporal relief he has his associations; for all who require spiritual
sustenance he has his missions and his retreats; for the
galley-slaves he has his special directors; for all criminals and prisoners he has a complete system of spiritual instruction.

Nor must we limit his work to what he achieved in
his own day. Like the Church whose faithful son he
ever was, his labours grew and prospered, and bore
fruit for future ages. Every work of his not only succeeded at first, not only lasted far beyond his time, but
now lives and flourishes as truly as when Vincent
guided it. The hardy plants which throve so well
have grown into lofty and wide-spreading trees, and
their seed has gone forth into all lands. France may
well glory in their birth; but every land rejoices in
their presence and profits by their fruit. The Lazarist
Father continues to preach the faith of Christ as well
to heathens as to unbelievers; he has his sojourn
among the Mahometans of the East, he penetrates into
the wilds of America, and into the equally unknown
regions of Thibet and China. The Sister of Charity
exercises her holy ministry, not only in the hospital
at Scutari, but amongst the mixed populations of
Constantinople, Alexandria, and Smyrna, and cheers
and comforts the sick-beds of our own Christian poor.
The spiritual retreat is given as regularly in this our
day as when St. Vincent conducted it in person; the
rule which he gave to his brethren continues to direct
their successors; the organisation which he devised
for the relief of the poor still prevails in most parts of

the world, exactly as when Madame Le Gras and her companions first entered upon the work in the days of Louis XIII.

And herein is our especial interest in the life here recorded. It comes home to ourselves and to our own times; for it tells of a work begun indeed upwards of two hundred years ago, but which is still going on in the midst of us. As the record of a life spent in deeds of active charity, it would have a claim upon our attention; as the beginning of a great movement for social amelioration, at a period of peculiar interest, when the feudal system was passing into the monarchical, and old forms and customs of society were breaking up, it would have an interest for the student of human nature and the lover of his race; but, over and above all this, it has that which takes it out of the past, and places it in the present, which removes it from the exclusive province of the historian, and brings it into the catalogue of living things, in which we have our part. St. Vincent de Paul still lives in his works; his spirit guides them now. He is not, then, merely one who lived with Louis and Henry of Navarre; who guided Richelieu in his choice of Bishops, and thwarted Mazarin in his misuse of power;—he ministers to our sick in the Crimea; he tells us of lands, of which, but for his disciples, we should know nothing; he walks our streets and relieves our poor; he warns the negligent and instructs the ignorant among us; he trains the priests who minister at our altars, and nurses the sick and wounded in our hospitals.

We cannot escape from Vincent de Paul. The energy of that dauntless old man cannot die; the love which burned so fervently in his heart is too divine ever to grow cold. Natural, then, it is that we should seek to know somewhat about him; that, if he will come among us, we may understand what he would be about; that, if he will have us work with him, we may know at what he is aiming, and of what spirit he is. The foregoing pages are designed to answer this inquiry. They seek only to set forth, plainly and simply, what others have already recorded at greater length and with more of detail. And if they kindle one holy aspiration, or induce to one act of charity, in imitation and through love of Him whom Vincent served so well, they will have gained their end.

O God, who didst strengthen blessed Vincent with apostolic courage to preach the Gospel to the poor, and promote the beauty of the ecclesiastical order; grant, we beseech Thee, that we who venerate his pious merits may also be instructed by the example of his virtues, through our Lord Jesus Christ Thy Son, who, with Thee, liveth and reigneth in the unity of the Holy Spirit, God, world without end. Amen.

THE END.